What the PA knew

An intriguing legal tale

LAW REPORTS

LAW REVIEW

CIVIL LAW

LEGAL DICTIONARY

DAWN DIXON

What the PA knew

First published in 2016 by

Panoma Press Ltd
48 St Vincent Drive, St Albans, Herts, AL1 5SJ, UK
info@panomapress.com
www.panomapress.com

Book design and layout by Neil Coe.

Printed on acid-free paper from managed forests.

ISBN 978-1-784520-81-6

The right of Dawn Dixon to be identified as the author of this work has been asserted in accordance with sections 77 and 78 of the Copyright, Designs and Patents Act 1988.

A CIP catalogue record for this book is available from the British Library.

This book is available online and in bookstores.

Dedication

My life has been a long and often at times difficult journey. It has taken many different twists and turns and ended up in some cul-de-sacs as well as one-way streets!

I wish to dedicate this book to a long-suffering group consisting of family, friends, professional advisers, colleagues and my dog, who have all supported me in their own individual ways during the last two years and since the untimely closure of my practice.

It sometimes takes a mammoth event in your life to make you want to document the things that have happened along the way, and for me it wasn't the closure of my firm but the way it happened and the realisation that I had no control over the situation. I felt that writing a book would help me to offset some of the emotion I was feeling and put it down on paper, relieving me of the anguish I felt inside.

I turned to The Book Midwife who has guided me through this process from beginning to end and with her support, belief and encouragement you are able to read this book today. The days were dark and the nights darker. The journey of this book started with a real event that gestated in my brain and was brought to life with the help and assistance of The Book Midwife.

I chose to write this book through the eyes of the many PAs/friends who have worked with me over the years. They have witnessed every personal and professional event in my life and continuously worked hard to make me look good in the eyes of the world by correcting my grammar and keeping my diary and my confidence and, of course, the confidence of clients and staff.

I know from first-hand experience that employers, solicitors in particular, can sometimes forget the work of the back office, forgetting that they truly are the ones that glue everything together and help not hinder you, and so writing this book through your eyes will help to relive the true events of my life through non biased eyes.

I would like to thank my parents for without them none of this would have been possible: my mum, Grace Deflorimonte and my father, Calbert Dixon. I would not want to forget the enormous contribution, help, assistance and love of my step-father Tony Deflorimonte. All three have helped make me who I am today.

I also wish to thank my sisters, Joanne Dixon and Nola-Jane Deflorimonte, who have made me laugh, cry and everything in between. They have made sure I did not take myself too seriously – ever! – and given me guidance with their down to earth criticism, and mainly their support.

I want to thank my nieces, Jolie and Sienna, and my nephew, Ethan, for being themselves. As children, they do not care what I do, as long as we have fun and I feed them.

Lastly I would like to thank Bella, my pet Labrador and best friend. On the days I just didn't feel like it, she followed me around and was there giving me love the only way a pet could – unconditionally. Our walks made me rethink my strategy and what was important in my life. She made sure I got out of the house, and if I didn't feel like it, she left deposits on the floor to remind me why I needed to go out three times a day!

How different life would have been if my parents had remained in the Caribbean and not ventured towards the west, where they met. Thank you to my lucky stars that brought them together and gave me life.

Acknowledgments

I wish to acknowledge the friends and family who have allowed me to use a little bit of their personalities to inject into my fictional characters – you know who are; and to those of you who have taught me the emotions of sadness, disappointment, betrayal and dismay because without you the inspiration for this book would remain untold.

Although many of the events recorded are factually and historically accurate, the names of the characters have been changed to protect the identity of those who may not want to be named and shamed.

I wish to personally thank my group of 'critics' who reviewed an early draft of this book. In no particular order: Grace Deflorimonte, Nola-Jane Deflorimonte, Joanne Dixon, Clare McConnell, O J Ebong, Judith McDermott, Dr Wayne Holness and Alison Parkinson.

I acknowledge all constructive criticism received by you which I have taken on board and hopefully produced a more readable account of my career.

Introduction

It is through lawyers that the public have access to justice. Not all members of the public can achieve justice themselves. So, the practice of law is a great and rewarding career, right? Isn't it? Think again. There is no 'personal specification' for a lawyer; they really are everyday people for everyday jobs. You must find your feet and fast. Not all of us are the fat cats we are perceived to be and as portrayed by documentaries, dramas and films.

It is with this background in mind that you should read this novel. It has been written through the (commentary) eyes of a PA (personal assistant) who has worked at the coalface of various legal firms and has often witnessed the growth of several careers during their own career. These people are the backbone of most offices and often at times the unsung heroes who are put upon by crazy, domineering, arrogant lawyers who are so convinced they are right as *"we know the law!"*

The PA can make a person – solicitor or otherwise – look good or bad. They type all-important memos, letters and documents which are top secret and confidential. They must keep their employer's confidences as well as those of the individual members of the firms and clients whose personal details they come across. They will have the front seat into the mind of an entrepreneurial lawyer and how that person was made.

Fionnula Egbo is a fictional character who has been friends with Diane since primary school through to middle and high school. They attended university together and both enrolled on a law degree course; however, upon completion of their education their lives take very different paths. Diane embarks on her desired legal career and Fionnula chooses to start a family alongside pursuing her chosen profession as a PA, as she wants to use her legal knowledge and typing skills together. Both enjoy the fruits of higher education without having to pay or borrow money. They were one of the last groups to receive local government help and support through the grants system. How times have changed.

They have remained firm friends and so this uniquely placed relationship spanning many decades helps us to understand the trials and tribulations that Diane faced on her journey through childhood, the start of her career and the events that led up to the closure of her pride and joy: her baby, her firm.

Foreword

What the PA knew gives a fascinating insight into what is commonly expected to be glitzy and sexy – the world of business and law – captured through the eyes of a sassy PA called Fionnula.

What the PA knew seamlessly combines a self-help guide burrowing its way through the pitfalls of a startup company with the busy life of Fionnula, a PA at a top law firm which boasts of being the first of its kind to have been established in the City of London, and the first of its kind to be a challenge to the 'Establishment' from within the City walls.

What the PA knew starts where two young girls from different backgrounds forge a bond at primary school that sees them through to adulthood. They plan on following the same path but life has a way of throwing those curve balls when we least expect it, and the two girls find themselves catapulted in opposite directions, yet friendship seems to win through.

You can't help but warm to Fionnula, the lead character, who tells her story of life, warts and all, reflecting on her own hopes and dreams. We all have those 'if onlys' stored away at the back of our minds and you won't be able to stop yourself from reaching out to Fionnula in empathy.

We follow Fionnula's story through the grinding challenges of working in a top City of London law firm while coping with love, family and friendship, many aspects of which will reach out and grab you.

The book winds itself up into a crescendo where all the elements come into play and culminates in a twist that you will never see coming!

A must-read book for any aspiring entrepreneurs or those who just like a good read.

Joanne Dixon

Contents

CHAPTER 1

Present Day

Gosh it's Friday and the first day of February 2013. The house is eerily quiet as I lie here in bed and ponder my life's journey. What a life! I am not Felicity Kendal in *The Good Life* but it isn't that bad either. I just like to complain – it's part of my DNA. I like a good controlled drama in my life if nothing else!

I am Fionnula Egbo (née O'Meara). Yep, an Irish/Nigerian mix. The name is a good one for starting up conversations. As I introduce myself, I can see people thinking *what, how does that work?* Well, easy really. My husband is Nigerian and I am from good old Irish stock. My parents came to England from Ireland in the 1960s.

I was born in 1966. The 1960s was a very strange time for racial integration in England and 40 years on, when you read about 'institutional racism' in various organisations, it feels like it's the same shit but a different decade. In the 1960s, I am told, there were signs in bed and breakfast windows advertising rooms but with the caveat 'No Blacks, No Irish, No dogs'.

We have always had dogs in the family home and there have always been Black people in the neighbourhoods I grew up in and it is therefore not surprising I married a Black man! I am Irish. I did not marry a Black Brit or someone of Caribbean origin. I married a Nigerian man, which is a very different type of Black person – or so my father says! I can't say I have noticed the difference. The Caribbean culture was assimilated into the British culture quite easily and they learnt to get on; but Africans have their own distinct language from Caribbean people's and their culture and heritage is very different from what I was used to growing up with in the Caribbean community.

My parents were not happy with me marrying an African as they seemed to think he was a world apart from the Caribbean people they knew from the 1960s. Anyway, hey ho, that's my parents' problem. I have been married for over 26 years. My parents are not exactly the norm either so they can Foxtrot Oscar! Pots and kettles spring to mind.

I feel really agitated today, I am not sure why.

As I am lying here, I start to think of my childhood. I went to St Bartholomew's Primary School in Wimbledon and I was put next to Diane Delaney. Both her parents are from the Caribbean. Her father is Jamaican and her mother is from Trinidad and Tobago. It always made me laugh that everyone assumed Trinidad was part of Jamaica whereas Trinidad is part of the two islands that make up Trinidad and Tobago. God, the world can be ignorant sometimes. Jamaica is not the capital of the Caribbean, it is a separate island. Diane often joked that when she went to Trinidad from Tobago by plane for the first time, the runway was so small that if they didn't hit the ground first time, you would fall off the other end of the island!

There were six chairs to a table at St Bartholomew's. Diane and I sat at a table together. There were some children who were late for the first day. A little boy with ginger hair came in and he said his name was John Pissy. Diane and I had a fit of giggles for the whole day every time we looked at him as, unfortunately, he smelt as if he had wet his bed and not changed his clothes. With my adult self lying here in bed I think *you're gonna go to hell for taking the piss out of John Pissy…* and I start laughing again. His name was too much for us to bear and with our childish selves we could not stop laughing. We were promptly sent to Mother Teresa, the headmistress, at the end of the day for laughing at John. By the time of the school bell, our parents had been told of the incident and we were in tears. We knew what was coming from our parents. Mine would be horrified, as they would think I had embarrassed them in front of a nun. As it happens, when I relayed the story to them they were angry, but not as much as I expected. Throughout our lives Diane and I would be laughing and crying constantly and in equal measures. That first day was obviously a very bad omen for the rest of our lives together as we continued to get into trouble.

Diane and I were both born in 1966 and think of ourselves as World Cup babies. My birthday is 13 July and Diane's is 16 July. We are both Cancerians and God help the world. Maybe that is why we get on so well. We recognise each other's mood swings, as Cancerians do so well, and are therefore well able to sidestep these moods which appear for no reason. Why can't our families recognise this? I ponder.

Diane always said that if her mother or father had moved west of the Caribbean to South America instead of east towards Europe, how different her life would have been. If my parents had stayed in Ireland, how different mine would have been. I would not have married my husband and had my children who are my world. I would be a traveller living in a caravan somewhere… maybe!

Diane and I separated at high school briefly. We came back together at university and the College of Knowledge, or the College of Law as most people called it, while doing our Law Society finals or the Cambridge Diet as it was referred to. Many of our classmates lost weight during that year as a result of the severity of the course. You had little time for play let alone to eat and sleep. By the end of the course there were 10–15 lever arch folders containing information we had to get from the folders into our heads in one go, for a very short period of time, to get us through the examination. It was pretty hard going.

How our lives have changed since. Diane became a young partner at 28 in a predominantly male practice. She then left and opened her own firm and ended up with over 3,000 square feet of space to pay for, several members of staff, various legal departments within the firm, and a big headache. Diane concentrated on her professional life. I married Francis Egbo on the 28th day of May 1990. We have four children: Francis Junior who is 25, Fiachra who is 20, Fiona who is 18 and Jack who I had in my 40s and who we lovingly refer to as Baby Boy. He is autistic and is five years old. We have a dog, Bella. She is a two-year-old black Labrador; she is our world and very spoilt but very affectionate and a pure joy. Jack loves to tell people she is a gun dog that her parents use to retrieve for farmers and she has two coats: one to keep her warm and one to keep her dry. That is our nuclear family.

Strange now that I am Diane's PA. Although we went to school together, our time apart at high school did not change our friendship one bit. Yes we have had our falling outs, as friends do. I loved English literature but decided to do law and followed Diane to Wolverhampton Polytechnic as it was called in the 1980s. My dad nearly had a heart attack when he realised he might have to pay for me during my time at Polytechnic and on the Law Society finals course. He was therefore relieved when the London

Borough of Merton agreed to fund me under the grants system. Diane's parents were divorced by then, so she was eligible for a full grant based on her mother's salary, which was allocated. I think we were the last of the students to receive the grant-aided assistance for the Law Society finals course. Now it costs a small fortune – equivalent to a mortgage.

I am a PA, with four children of various ages, whose best friend owns her own firm. My husband is a struggling solicitor/author. I am telling this story, as Diane and I are like glue. We have always stuck together and will continue to do so. Her dad used to call us Batty and Brief in his Jamaican patois as we could not get any closer than a bum and its briefs. We were inseparable. I knew what she was thinking even before she said it and vice versa. Therefore, it is quite apt for me to tell her story. I was there with her almost every step of the way. I have lived her life... or it feels like that, and therefore I feel well qualified as her friend, confidante, employee and colleague to tell her story and impart her knowledge. We are like family.

I decided to be Diane's PA for the simple reason that she allowed me to work flexibly. She knew my family and its various machinations from inception and she grew up with us all. She even calls my dad Uncle Pops, which is just typical for her to make up some complete nonsense. How can someone be your uncle and your father/pops?

Diane was a good boss. If I couldn't come into the office at short notice, she did not mind... too much. She eventually set up a system where I could work remotely from home. Due to his autism and resulting problems, Jack has some days where he just does not want to cooperate with life and I have had to work from home. Most employers would not allow this, but as Diane is Jack's godmother, she either does not mind or does not say that she minds.

As I lie here in bed, I think of how Diane and I separated at high school. I remember it was initially my own snobbery that stopped us talking for a few months. I thought I was better than Diane because I was going to Wandle High and Diane was going to Ursula Convent; I had passed my 11-plus so I felt I was somehow better than her. How stupid can you be? I am almost embarrassed as I think about this. We both passed the 11-plus; the difference was her father would not pay the school fees, not that I was brighter than her.

During the early years when my three older children went to school, I had problems with a lot of my bosses. Solicitors can be quite difficult to work with. I was at their beck and call. I was always the first to be made redundant. If there were any issues with the children's health, I had to take time off, so was not viewed as a safe pair of hands for a business owner. Looking back, I took far too much time off and was almost working flexibly before flexible working was as widely used as it is today. I wouldn't employ me! Law firms are forward thinking in some respects but definitely inflexible in relation to flexible working – if you know what I mean. It took them a long time to get it. It's a blessing that I can work as I do now. Even though I had known Diane for years and most staff knew that, I still had to make an application to work flexibly as Diane insisted that we had to be seen to be fair to all. Justice must not only be done but it must be seen to be done.

It is true that you need to spend time with friends who see you cry and not just those who see you laugh. Those friends who see your tears see the real you. Diane has seen my tears and she has also seen my laughter and my drunken hysteria to boot! After leaving the College of Law, Diane was eventually admitted to the Roll of Solicitors and I was admitted to hospital with my first child, Francis Junior.

What's the noise? Actually there is no noise at all and that is why it is making me so nervous today. Oh shit, I haven't let Bella out into the garden for a wee! That bloody dog has probably pooed on the floor and weed on top just to make her point. As I swing my legs out of the bed I look at the clock and nearly have heart failure. It is nearly 7.30am and the whole house is still quiet. Where is Francis? Why hasn't Bella come into the bedroom and jumped on the bed as she normally does, stupid dog? I curse and again say, "I am taking that dog to Battersea Dogs & Cats Home," but I know I won't. I get up to check on Fiona who is due at college and Francis Junior and Fiachra who are due at work. All I can see is legs and arms in their rooms. I am now beginning to wonder whether these young adults will ever be self-reliant. Why are they still in my home for goodness' sake? I rap on the doors loudly to wake them all up and then go and check on Baby Boy who is washed and dressed. It is his first full term at a new school and he is still very excited. I look at my little man in awe. We called him Jack as we knew something was wrong with the pregnancy from early on. All members of the family have a Christian name starting with F but we thought Jack was going to be different and he is, so we gave him a different initial. He always thinks it is funny that his name starts with a different initial from everyone else in the family but we told him it was because he is so special. He now tells everyone he is more special than other members of the family. We tell him that we wanted him because he was going to be special. As I look at him now, washed and dressed and with the others still wandering around banging into each other, I think he is probably the most sensible person in the household. He helps me get the others up and ready for the day.

As I fall out of the shower and into my clothes, I head downstairs to get some food and fall into the kitchen. Neither Francis Senior nor Bella are anywhere to be seen. Eureka! Now I feel really guilty. Shit. It is Friday and Francis starts work late on Fridays and always takes Bella for a walk first. On all the other days Bella is walked by my neighbour, Laura. Why the hell didn't the alarm go off? I realise there was a power surge in the night and the radio alarm clock went back to zero, it did not reset. I leave myself a mental note to replace that thing ASAP.

Francis comes back in with Bella. He looks relaxed. She looks knackered and does not want her breakfast as she slumps on the kitchen floor exhausted with her tongue hanging out of the side of her mouth and very close to her ear. Francis then admits that he took her round the park but rather than walking, he cycled while she ran next to him on the lead. I am so annoyed as we have had this discussion many times, that he needs to build up the dog's stamina rather than try to kill her before she is one year old. She is still a puppy! I leave the house in a huff. We have always had dogs in the home and I know how to look after them. Francis had dogs in Nigeria as a child but they were never house dogs, they were always yard dogs and never pets in the home the way we have them in England. In Jamaica, Diane says, they have dogs and in England we have pets.

Francis can clear up the mess of the three older children and he will be taking Jack to school. I get to the bus stop and all I can see is the bus moving off in the distance. Shit. I am exhausted with my life. I am tired of being sick and sick of being tired. As I turn the corner, another bus appears and I get to the underground station and the train pulls off as I am just about to run down the stairs. Shit, I say for the umpteenth time today and it isn't even 8.30am.

I get off the train at Chancery Lane and have to resist the urge not to go into McDonalds for a breakfast meal – my second breakfast of the day. I must lose weight and McDonalds will not help in this quest! I am not sure why I have a knot in my stomach and I don't think food is going to fill it.

I move a little faster as I manage to make up a bit of time notwithstanding my morning and I am only 15 minutes late as I start at 9.30am. As I cross Holborn Circus and get closer to the building I can't shake off how uncomfortable I feel; it's as if something is about to happen. I nip into Lloyds Bank quickly as I need some cash and I know that if I leave it until lunchtime there will be far too many people milling around and winding me up during my hour's break. I don't want to waste that hour in the bank.

As I turn the corner into the Taylor Court entrance, there are police cars outside the building.

I say hello to Peter, the doorman. He looks tired. I think to myself he needs a holiday. Mind you, so do I. Peter always reminds me of Father Ted. It is not because of his grey hair or the fact he does actually wear a cardigan, it's his Irish accent. It gets me every time. He doesn't say anything to me apart from, "Morning." As I get into the lift, he has a pensive look on his face and I wonder *what the hell is wrong with him today?* He is not his normal cheery self. As the lift ascends all I can hear is raised voices. I get off at the eighth floor, which I lovingly refer to as the penthouse suite and, oh shit (there's that word again), there are police in the office. What the hell has just happened?

CHAPTER 2

1960–1985

LAW REPORTS

LAW REVIEW

CIVIL LAW

LEGAL DICTIONARY

I believe that in order for you to understand where you are going, you need to know where you have come from. If you don't know where you are coming from, or recognise that the past shapes your future, you could be lost forever and never learn life's lessons – whatever they may be and however they come to you.

Declan O'Meara, my dad, is of good old Irish stock. His family have lived in Kilkenny for years. His father, grandfather and great grandfather before him had owned public houses in the Kilkenny area. Declan did not want to go into the family business and decided to get on a boat from Cork to Fishguard, as the Dublin to Liverpool route would have taken him up towards the north of England where he had no living relatives at the time of his travels. The boat was called *The Pride of Ireland* and he was proud of himself that he was on his journey to find his way in the world and, he felt, become his own man.

Declan was the youngest of 13 children and found it difficult to find his own way with so many siblings and the rivalries that inevitably ensued. He could see his future would be looking at the bottom of glasses, either drinking or collecting them, and he decided at 16 the best route for him was to get the first boat out of Ireland.

He travelled to England in 1959 with his father's blessing. While on the crossing, he came across a Romany family (travellers/tinkers to you). Three young male travellers (whom he referred to as the 'Tree Trunks') in their early 20s were travelling with a younger female relative. They were accompanying this 15-year-old girl who, Declan found out, was called Bridget. He didn't know her surname. She was on her way to England to live with relatives. The travelling community would never have allowed her to travel to England unaccompanied so the Tree Trunks guarded her virtue. Declan did not know the circumstances of her move to England, but something had happened to make her family agree to her leaving Ireland. Declan always recalled how enamoured he was with Bridget who looked like a handful, but he was more scared of her than her three minders who were so big, he said, that they would have measured nearly 19 feet if you laid them out head to toe! Declan was 5 foot 7.

Around this time, the travelling community in Ireland never mixed with the settled Irish community. Declan thought talking to Bridget would have risked his life for sure, but looking at her from a distance couldn't be all that bad. He tried to figure out a way of talking to her, but every time he got close one of her 'minders' assumed a position right next to her. When he later retold the story, he always said that they would 'strike a pose', but their pose was more of a grimace and very frightening. He never got his wish to speak with her. As a 16-year-old impressionable young man, he fell in love with Bridget on sight, even though they had never exchanged a word. Stupid romantic fool. The journey only lasted a few hours, but the impression lasted a lifetime as he continued to watch Bridget from a distance, but didn't get the opportunity to exchange a single word with her.

The tinkers went to North London to meet their family and Declan settled in the Clapham Junction area. He had an uncle who lived on Burgess Road, St John's Hill, Clapham. Seamus O'Meara, or Uncle Seamus, had a four-storey house which he rented out on a room-by-room basis as was the norm at that time. Some rooms were shared by shift workers. When one group was at work, the others were sleeping and vice versa, and in the same beds which had 24-hour occupancy, always in use. It was fair to say that Uncle Seamus was doing very well, but he had no wife or children. He took Declan under his considerably large wing – Uncle Seamus was very overweight. Declan moved in with him in 1959 and found out that Uncle Seamus was known by the children in the neighbourhood as Seamus the Leprechaun on account of his lack of height. He should have been a jockey but he was far too overweight and would have flattened a horse anyway! Uncle Seamus had also run away from the pubs of Kilkenny and so he had a soft spot for Declan who was trying to do the same thing as him, but at a much younger age, and Uncle Seamus felt obliged to protect and help out his young nephew.

When landing on the streets of London, Declan walked everywhere so as to familiarise himself with his surroundings. It was a lot more confusing than Kilkenny, which in comparison was small. He was shocked to see that bed and breakfasts up and down Clapham/Brixton/ south London displayed signs stating that 'No Blacks, No Irish and No dogs' were welcome – but not in Uncle Seamus's house. He welcomed anyone with money as money had one colour! Declan, being a bit of a racist himself insofar as there were very few African-Caribbean or African people in Ireland in the 1950s, did not have any objection to being likened to a dog, but he did object to being likened to Black people. It is ironic, therefore, that it was the same Black families that he grew up with in Clapham in the 1960s that became his nearest and dearest for life, and his drinking buddies.

It was early 1960 and 17-year-old Declan met Cuthbert Delaney who was a 16-year-old fresh from Jamaica, West Indies. For the first few months Cuthbert and Declan were inseparable. In fact they looked very much alike – apart from the fact that one had a very strong Jamaican accent and a slight tint. Declan was slightly darker for a White man and Cuthbert slightly lighter for a Black man and therefore they merged and looked like kin. Cuthbert moved in with his father Daniel Delaney in Burgess Road and met Declan. Daniel used to drink with Uncle Seamus in the local pubs. Declan and Cuthbert would often be seen outside, nursing what everyone believed to be apple juice but was in fact a lager shandy. They both regrettably grew to like the taste of alcohol and, at some times, far too much!

Cuthbert was looking for a job and Declan was hustling for Uncle Seamus. They both then started to hustle together and got into some minor scraps with the police, usually for selling alcohol that Cuthbert mixed, which was the equivalent of American moonshine. It was Jamaican rum called John Crow Batty or Kulu Kulu. Declan worked with Uncle Seamus in his building business and roped in Cuthbert wherever he could for labouring work, which paid cash in hand. They did this for a few months and on the eve of Declan's 18th birthday decided to go out and celebrate in style.

In those days if you lived in south London you went to the Hammersmith Palais. It was expensive to get in and Declan and Cuthbert spent a lot of money impressing the ladies and buying everyone drinks. They then checked their pockets only to realise they had no money for a cab home. They therefore had to walk from Hammersmith to Clapham, which took over two hours. They never minded, however, because they were wearing their whiskey coats and could not feel the cold.

Declan had never forgotten Bridget and when Cuthbert was seen 'stepping out' regularly with a Smallie, i.e. someone from a 'small island', Declan decided it was time for him to look for a partner of his own. He remembered Bridget and started to look for Irish travelling families in the north London area, but they were so secretive as a group, they were not registered anywhere and his search proved fruitless. He did not know enough travelling families to be able to make enquiries as too many questions in the wrong place could lead to him losing his teeth. He didn't even know her surname, for God's sake.

It was purely by chance that Cuthbert, his new girlfriend Gwendolyn and Declan went to the annual fair on Wimbledon Common. Declan could not believe his luck: Bridget was standing by the Ferris wheel. He stared and stared. He thought the gods were playing a trick on his eyesight and his brain was not registering what his eyes were telling him he was seeing. But it was her, and although she was dwarfed by a very large dark-haired hairy man with huge muscles and more tattoos than he'd ever seen, he summoned up enough courage this time to go over and speak with her, regardless of the Tree Trunks.

Bridget, of course, feigned ignorance that she had ever seen him as it would not be good for her to be associated with a member of the Irish settled community. Declan later learnt this was exactly what got her into trouble in the first place and why she was sent to England by her father.

Never mind, thought Declan. He persevered and somehow managed to win over the family. Declan is very charming and many say typical of an Irishman who has kissed the Blarney Stone.

There was an accident on the Ferris wheel that same evening. For reasons best known to Seamus and the gods, he wanted Declan to learn first aid for the business. Declan thought it was for sissies; however, to keep the peace and to keep Uncle Seamus from arguing, decided to do the course. Although the accident on the Ferris wheel was not major, Declan was able to make the individual comfortable until the paramedics arrived and stopped the bleeding. The Tree Trunks were very impressed and that evening took Declan out to the Crooked Billet pub on the common for a drink to say thank you. Declan tried to remain sober as he was scared he may have blurted out how much he liked Bridget. Cuthbert and Gwendolyn looked as if they had stopped breathing. The Tree Trunks were so thankful they ignored Declan's stares at Bridget.

Declan was a hard worker and involved the Tree Trunks and their families in the labouring game with Uncle Seamus, where they received cash in hand and no questions were asked. Declan was in good favour with them and he felt comfortable enough to start talking to Bridget. He was promptly beaten up by the Tree Trunks... but not too badly and just so they could tell the family that they had dealt with him.

Eighteen months later he had set up home with Bridget and he had no idea who in the family had prevented the Tree Trunks, their brothers, uncles and offspring from putting him in hospital or permanently taking a dirt nap.

The first time he spoke to Bridget he was so scared he wondered if he would wake up in casualty and ask the nurse how long the Tree Trunks had put him in a coma! Bridget was about to give birth to their child, Grainne. Cuthbert had also got married about that time and was eagerly awaiting the birth of his first child, a son.

I think that our parents, Diane's and mine, came from very different backgrounds but still seemed to get on so well together as basically they were all good honest people. Cuthbert, I understand, was from a place in Jamaica called St Elizabeth, where the population is as White as their Scottish and Irish ancestors. He left school at a very young age and was taught to read by my father when they met in London. His wife came from Trinidad and Tobago where it is said they dance when they walk and sing when they talk. She arrived in the UK at the age of 17 and was living with an older brother, Albert, in Clapham. Years later I was taken to the Notting Hill Carnival with Diane and her mother and we were walking down Ladbroke Grove when all of a sudden Gwendolyn asked us to dart into a shop. Two rather confused girls did as they were told, as this strapping young coolie man walked past with what was odd in those days, tattoos all over his chest. Diane's mum turned to us and said that she would recognise that man anywhere. The day she left Trinidad she had agreed to meet him in Port of Spain just to get him off her case as he wanted to take her out. She knew that at the appointed time of the meet she would be at Piarco Airport on a BWIA flight bound for London.

With all of their joint history, it is not surprising Declan and Cuthbert moved from Clapham to Battersea and then from Battersea to Wimbledon together. In fact our homes were on Haydons Road, right next to Plough Lane, the home of Wimbledon FC who later won the FA Cup against Liverpool.

Inevitably, Diane and I went to the same primary school. Diane was a strange child. She never spoke at school although she spoke too much at home. Thankfully we were put next to each other on the first day. We looked so different: I was White, Diane was Black, I was blonde, Diane was dark, I was short, Diane was tall. My dad referred to us as the long and short of it all!

Diane was too serious for a child but she was studious, and I remember she was able to read before we went to school. It was odd that my father was able to read and Cuthbert not, and Diane could read before she started school but I could not.

It was a Monday morning and the teacher became pretty frustrated with something and Diane did not help the situation. All the children were in a queue waiting to read for the form teacher. True to form, Diane would not speak and certainly would not read for the teacher. Miss Gonzalez, our form teacher, thought Diane was either deaf or backward. I had no idea what autism was back then and it is curious that Baby Boy is now on that very same spectrum they thought Diane was.

Anyway Diane was not deaf, backward or autistic. She was told to stand behind the teacher and, for her punishment, to wait until the entire class had read their books for the teacher so she could witness how good children behaved. However, Miss Gonzalez' plan backfired. As the other children were struggling with their words and their books, Diane mouthed the correct word to them, to Miss Gonzalez' frustration. It was clear to all that Diane was able to read, she just did not want to read for the teacher. Later, when asking Diane why she behaved that way, she just said she did not like the teacher. However, Miss Gonzalez would have her day. She reported Diane to the headmistress and said she was an obstructive child and disrupted the natural routine of the class – whatever. She felt Diane needed to have her ears tested as she believed Diane to be deaf. Furthermore, Miss Gonzalez felt Diane had an attitude problem, which, when you think about it – for God's sake, we were five years old! Never judge a book by its cover I say, or not at least until you have read some pages. Diane's mum protested to the school proclaiming that her daughter was not deaf, that clearly there was nothing wrong with her ears and that she had the best hearing in the household. She was certain something else was the cause of Diane's silence.

However, to appease the teachers, Gwendolyn took Diane to a specialist who promptly told Gwendolyn it was a waste of his time and Diane was just strong willed and did not like the teacher and therefore would not cooperate with her. There was nothing wrong with her or her ears. There was a meeting between Diane's parents and Miss Gonzalez and it was agreed that Diane would be moved to another class with a stricter form teacher. That would not happen today in 2015. Teachers may not get the support from family and school and would be told to sink or swim. Children have more power today and parents more say. Suffice to say, Diane was moved to 1B and away from Miss Gonzalez; I remained in 1A.

On the first day in 1B Diane was so nervous as she had met Mrs Fernandez who was married to a South American. She was from Barbados. She was not going to take any crap from a five-year-old child who she felt should be 'seen and not heard'. As it was now established that Diane could hear, speak and read, she was given the task of having to perform in front of the class on a daily basis until she understood that when asked to do something in class by the teacher she would do it, and not question the teacher's authority. Even at this young age she was a miserable sod. She was so frightened of Mrs Fernandez that she was constipated for the first two days and sent home early. She never missed a day at school after that.

Until we attended middle school there was nothing remarkable that happened in our lives. I proceeded through A-stream and Diane through B-stream. The classes were not separated by ability. All children of different abilities were lumped together in the same class, but inevitably in 1977 we both took the 11-plus and, bloody hell, we both passed! We were offered grant-maintained places at Wandle High School for Girls. Mum thought it amusing that she had actually stayed in one place for several years despite her early roving background and now she had a daughter who was going to a grammar school. What would the saints say? Mum and Dad agreed to pay the extra fee to top up the grant so the full fee was paid.

Diane's dad, Cuthbert, however, was so tight he squeaked when he walked. He had no real formal education himself. He felt it was unnecessary to pay for a child's education when state schools were free. I think Diane would have been resentful had she not made anything of her own life, but she did well regardless of her father's ignorance and short pockets. Cuthbert needed to learn not to judge people by his own standards. He did not want to spend any money because no one spent any money on his education and he felt he had done OK with his life – even if that was debatable.

I continued with my education at Wandle High School and met up with Diane and her family in the evenings and at weekends as we both still lived in South Wimbledon.

Diane went to Ursula Convent in Wimbledon at the age of 13. She enjoyed it both academically and socially. One April Fool's Day as a laugh, she told me, a group of girls she knew put cling film over the nuns' private toilets and they all waited for the screams of displeasure. The girls responsible received a detention and were nearly expelled. The convent was a very good Catholic school in Wimbledon at the time. Diane did OK in her exams, not great. She was moved up in the first year from the middle stream to the top stream. The convent operated a very distinct educational stream system based on ability. She was bright but lazy and easily led. However, on reaching 16 and falling into the hands of the careers officer, she decided to let them know that she wanted to practise law, the same as me. She was told by the careers officer that as a member of an ethnic group she was setting her standards too high! I am still shocked when I think about this today and thank God things have moved on. Now that was like a red rag to a bull. I don't know whether educational establishments realised just how much they affected lives.

Diane's brother Martin wanted to become an electronics engineer but he was told to become a motor mechanic.

He is now the director of an energy company. Go figure! Later, when Diane opened her firm, she went back to the convent and asked the girls to design a logo for her practice. She printed off the logo and placed it in a frame, which included a sample letterhead, business card and compliments slip, and gave it to the winning designer. She also gave a donation to the convent. I suppose in her way it was self-satisfying. She did not want to get upset with the comment that was made so many years ago and although she forgave it she never forgot it. She got even in her head and it felt good. The school never thought she would make anything of herself but she made sure that she told them in her unique way that she had.

Even in those early days, we knew Diane was going to be argumentative. I used to meet her in Wimbledon town centre after school and on one occasion she was late. Quite regularly, Ursula Convent (or Virgins on the Hill) would meet up with The Lodge (Scrubbers Lodge) for an impromptu debacle in Wimbledon town centre, which often ended up in a real fight. I supported Ursula Convent as I knew most of the girls who had gone to my primary and middle school and were hanging around in Wimbledon. I had to change my school uniform so I would not be recognised as an outsider. Diane was late this particular day and when she turned up she was angry and confessed that she and the whole class had received a detention. She was talking in class – no surprise there then! Her teacher, Miss Burke, seemed to zero in on Diane speaking. Diane complained that the whole class was talking and asked whether Miss Burke had antennas for her mouth only. Miss Burke was not impressed with this comment... naturally. She asked Diane to write out various Psalms from the Bible as punishment during and after school that day. Being the junior lawyer Diane was to become, she said that the Bible should not be used as a form of punishment and she did not accept what Miss Burke had proposed as the punishment which she felt was wrong and disproportionate in the circumstances. For being a precocious prat, the entire class received detention; however, what was even worse was that Miss Burke blamed Diane's behaviour as a reason for the entire class being punished. The class did not blame Diane, though, they felt Diane was right and as good Catholic girls objected to the unholy use of the Holy Book.

Miss Burke had wanted to alienate Diane from the class, but it backfired. She believed that if the class felt the punishment to be Diane's fault, next time she talked in class they would tell her to be quiet. The detention reached the ears of Mother Superior who had quietly agreed with Diane but did not say so in public. We never saw Miss Burke after that, and Diane became something of a legend in that she had stood up to a teacher, although the teachers themselves would not agree to this version of events.

By this time, Diane was 5 foot 7 and very sporty. She was as tall as all the teachers so they were defensive in her presence. All the girls, however, thought her to be quite cool. Diane was the youngest in the class but every Friday evening when we all met up in Wimbledon Village, she was the one who was sent to buy the drinks in the pubs because of her height. She continued, however, to have problems with teachers throughout her academic career.

A teacher in the 1970s had power and control. It seems that the tables have turned 180 degrees today. Now 14-year-old children are over 6 foot and teachers are unable to tell them off the way we were, or indeed reprimand them for fear of breaching their human rights. Crikey, in the 1970s students received the cane for goodness' sake – blow their human rights! How did we manage to move so far in the opposite direction? There is no more cane. I say bring back National Service. In the 1970s, if you misbehaved you got your knuckles rapped. Not now, you would get sued by the parents and the local authority would look upon such behaviour as barbaric. It did not upset our education or progression at all. When did we suddenly realise that children now have more human rights and laws to protect them? It sort of just crept up. Since we were at school, there appear to be more and more laws for the protection of children, which is quite right but it appears to have come back and bitten us all on the backside. I wouldn't be a teacher now for all the tea in China.

The system, however, did pick up very early that Baby Boy was on the autistic spectrum and the SENCO (Special Educational Needs Coordinator) at school liked him and looked after him well. On his first day at school he kicked his teacher. The teachers could not accept that sort of behaviour but realised it was the first day and that he was perhaps overexcited. When I asked him why he did so he told me that the teacher was in his way! It made me think of Diane and not reading for the teachers. Some children can just be bloody-minded!

In those days, if you were a little odd then you were a little odd and you had to fend for yourself. I know many children who had left school and weren't able to read and write as they somehow managed to slip through the net.

Surely that would lead to a parent suing the local authority today.

These days things are very different as special needs are recognised and diagnosed early and we have special educational needs coordinators in schools.

We all firmly believe that Baby Boy's autism may have been a result of having him in my 40s. There is a big argument today that it is bad for the foetus for women to have children in their 40s, but I had previously given birth to three children. Although I had a test which suggested that the foetus might be abnormal, Francis and I decided to proceed with the pregnancy to full-term anyway. But look at him now! The only thing he does not like is eye contact. Aunty Diane told him not to look at people's eyes but their eyebrows as it was less intrusive and uncomfortable. Now no one knows any different. But what a character! He is the funniest little man I know.

I suppose life isn't in a pretty box with a special label addressed to you and a bow. It is a gift and we need to treasure it and open it and use it. Lord, I'm beginning to sound like my mother!

I remember Diane and my first legal outing while at school; Diane and I went on a trip to the Old Bailey during the summer holidays. When she got there it was slightly later than the start time and as she went up the stairs she asked the guard whether there were any good cases on that we should be sitting in on. The guard looked at Diane and said under his breath to his colleague, "One of your family members is in Court 6." Diane had heard him and knew what he meant. She presumed there was a Black defendant in Court 6. I was surprised that Diane did not react until she got halfway down the corridor. She promptly turned around and went back to the guard and said, "Actually, not one member of my family has ever been in trouble with the police and certainly has not yet appeared at the Old Bailey as a defendant. And neither has any family member worked as a doorman for a living!" That shut the guards up! Over lunch Diane vowed never to step foot in the Old Bailey again. I wondered if she would be able to keep that promise.

CHAPTER 3

University: 1980s

Crikey, 1988! Wimbledon FC has just won the FA Cup final, OMG, and what a year it has been! The Crazy Gang, as Wimbledon FC were called, and a crazy year. Both Diane and I took our A levels. We got reasonable grades, which enabled us to get into Wolverhampton Polytechnic (one of the few Polytechnics that offered an LLB (Hons) in those days) which is now a university.

Wolverhampton was picked way before we even took our A Levels because it was not too close to London, but not far away enough that if we had to get back home in a rush it was not a cumbersome journey. It was only a two-hour journey to Euston station then a further hour home to south London. Bristol, Birmingham and Manchester were also viewed and rejected before we settled on Wolverhampton as the distance was acceptable. All we now needed was to go on a tour.

Diane and I went on a field trip to Wolverhampton and wandered around the area. We liked what we saw and we applied for places on our UCCA forms. Wolverhampton was quite depressed in those days, but we did not care. Students were living mainly in the Whitmore Reams area which was deprived, and drugs and prostitution (including child prostitution) were rife. We were both lucky, however, and secured rooms at Broadway Hall in Dudley, some miles from Wolverhampton.

The day we arrived at Broadway Hall was a bad omen, I think. It was cold. It was damp. It was a disgustingly miserable day. Dudley Hall was a very old house opposite Dudley Zoo and the Magistrates' Court. When we had visited the Midlands in the summer, it was a bright and sunny day. On this cold and damp day in September it didn't look as appealing. The first night was the worst. We met some nice people, but it was the first time we had both been away from our families, and as the younger of the two of us, Diane was already homesick and could barely eat. We managed to make it through freshers' week and promptly returned to London and back to what we thought was civilisation – central heating and carpets!

Diane's mother had remarried by then and Diane had a younger sister, Nora-Jean who was three months old. Diane had looked after Nora-Jean during the summer and on returning home after a fortnight in Wolverhampton Nora-Jean would not go to her. She just screamed like Diane was hurting her. Diane thought that a child's memory was so short that it really upset her, and she vowed she would not be returning to Wolverhampton if Nora-Jean could so easily forget her after a few weeks.

The following morning Gwendolyn woke Diane up at 6.30am and gave her Nora-Jean to feed, and after that feed it was as if Nora-Jean remembered who Diane was. Suffice to say she returned with me to Wolverhampton and after that she had to make a point of speaking with her sister constantly as a baby, so she would keep recognising her voice. This would backfire on Diane in later life as Nora-Jean has had various periods of living at Diane's home as an adult, on her own, with her partner and her daughter and latterly with all of them and their dog!

Wolverhampton Polytechnic was an eye-opener. I had never seen so many Asian faces in one place in my life. We did some interesting things and met some interesting people. For our sins we would later attend the Molineux Stadium on Saturday afternoons to watch Wolverhampton

Wanderers attempt to play football. Not very exciting but it was just something to do.

During freshers' week we had our first taste of lectures. The head of the Law School addressed us on the first day – Mr Robertson. It was, by all accounts, a larger class than usual. He was clear not all of us would pass. Some of us would end up with a third-class degree if we didn't work, and many would end up with a 2:2, but only a few of us would get a first or 2:1. He wanted us to think, work hard and decide which group we thought we would fit into at the end of the three years. While he was talking and spouting his knowledge about the law, I remembered Declan's philosophy: people who can't do, teach! I wondered if the lecturers still practised law. I think some were failed barristers/solicitors. I was looking around the auditorium.

We were in the Midlands and there was a predominance of Asian students but what actually caught my eye was a group of Nigerian students at the front of the lecture hall. There were at least two rows of Nigerian students all huddled together. I now know they all came from different parts of Nigeria, but they had all gravitated towards each other. I suppose there was security in numbers and nothing like what you know to feel secure. They viewed Diane as strange as they were not sure if she was Black or White. In fact, they viewed anyone who was not Nigerian as weird. I absentmindedly started talking to them as we were all in the lecture hall waiting for the next speaker. What I didn't realise was that one of them was looking right back at me. I later knew him to be Francis Egbo, but would never have understood his significance at that time.

Diane struck up a conversation with the Nigerians who let on that there was a house selling 'provisions'. It sold yam, green banana, sweet potato etc. at very reasonable prices. It was only available to Afro-Caribbean students and part of the Afro-Caribbean society's perks for its members. Diane located the address and we decided that we would venture into the Whitmore Reams area to find the shop together, but I was not to go into the shop with her.

I always remembered Diane's mum cooking fried plantain on a Sunday morning and so had a vested interest in going with Diane. I wondered if she could also get some salt fish to make saltfish and bake. Then I remembered she wasn't a great cook. Diane made it through the front door but came out five minutes later, visibly very upset. She said that as she entered the building she was stopped by a burly-looking Rastafarian asking her where she thought she was going. She confirmed that she was there to buy provisions. She was promptly told that the establishment only served Afro-Caribbean students. Diane was confused and speechless. She confirmed that both her parents were of Caribbean origin but she was told to leave anyway. It was bizarre as in all the years that I had known Diane never had she been discriminated against by another Black person. This man must have had a problem as it is obvious Diane is not of White complexion, and it could be questioned if she is Black or mixed-race. She could be mistaken for Middle Eastern, but only at a stretch, and in a very dark room. Her hair was far too curly and although she is not the darkest person you would see she is certainly not White and I was left thinking was this man a true Rasta man or some fraud? Surely he would have understood the implications of slavery, which accounts for the 32 shades of the Afro-Caribbean community. Why did he behave so appallingly towards Diane? There must be another reason or, seriously, he was having a bad day.

Diane was vexed. All day, she was in the foulest of moods that I had ever seen her in the time we had known each other. We turned the corner to go back to the Law Library and walked straight into Nelson and Chika, two Nigerian students on the course. Diane relayed her story to them and they were speechless as they knew the Rasta man on the door and thought he was OK. They agreed to walk back to the place with us as they often bought food from there and in true Nigerian fashion 'cussed off' the Rastafarian from his head to his foot for treating one of their 'sisters' like that. It was a very strange experience being a witness to the dynamics of two very young and angry African men against a middle-aged Rastafarian who seemed to have somehow become confused all of a sudden, and with Diane in the middle thinking *what the hell has just happened?*

The Nigerian men on the course thought they were the 'Italians' of Africa and I think they would have supported any female in trouble if they thought it would help them personally and score a favour with the ladies. These two were very secretive young men but became good friends of ours. It was not until some time later we learnt that Chika was sleeping with a local Brummie girl on the course who I would never have believed would have been interested in Chika. They never spoke in the library, they never sat next to each other. In fact they appeared totally indifferent to each other. The fact they were together is irrelevant, the fact Chika chose to hide it was what was curious to me. They never exchanged glances; they were on speaking terms but anything else, no way!

The Nigerian women were a different kettle of fish entirely. The women were often very rude to Diane as well as others, but seemed to tolerate me. It was some time before we realised that they were concerned about Diane and the other West Indian women on the course because they incorrectly, I think, felt their Nigerian men/African men would look at these women in a better light than their own. I learnt in those very early years that Nigerian/African culture accepted West Indians because they expected West Indians to behave in a particular way, as they were of the firm belief that all West Indians are African anyway because of their heritage, or so Diane was told when she asked. They don't expect the White community to understand African culture and so expect less from us and put up with more from us because of our perceived ignorance, which bore no resemblance to reality. A Caribbean woman who married an African man had to conform. A White woman who married an African did not. I later found out this would not be the case in my household.

This may very well be so, but with Diane's Jamaican father I have come to learn that Jamaicans and Nigerians are actually very similar in temperament. They are only separated by an ocean and a language. They are good, bad, loud and unruly in exactly the same quantities. When Chika and Nelson were supporting their 'sister' they probably were, in their minds. That being the case, why were the women so different?

Diane and I were waiting outside the Law Library for it to open one morning when Jessica came in. Jessica is not her real name, but her English assumed name. I cannot recall her Nigerian name. We got into a heated discussion about the African and Caribbean 'question' as Jessica put it. Diane felt there needed to be a conversation between both communities as to the existence of the perceived or otherwise distrust over the slave trade and its effects on both groups. Diane was fair-minded, but it wasn't just the Nigerian women on the course, it was also her own family who were inherently racist. Her Jamaican grandparents have always said to her that "nuttin too black ain't no good." I could never understand it as prejudice was always presented to me anyway and in the media as Black on White and vice versa when really it wasn't that simple. Everyone is capable of prejudice.

It was a shock then when Jessica whispered that the reason some Nigerian women on the course did not like Caribbean women was not only because of their lighter complexion and straighter hair, on which they are unable to compete, but more seriously and on a very negative undertone, they firmly believed these people were 'slave babies'. There were no West Indian men on the course at the time, but it was applied to them, too. I was horrified. Diane gave nothing away but I could tell she was seething. She looked at Jessica and smiled and said that may be so but, as far as she was concerned, she had never sold one member of her family yet! That put an end to that conversation and we never had a discussion with Jessica, or indeed any of the other Nigerian women, about this topic again.

Chika and Nelson decided they were going to have a party. Everyone was invited. The Nigerians, Caribbeans, the White students, the Asian students and the Chinese students. It was a real United Nations and something I had never really experienced before. Although many of the Asian students professed they did not drink because of their religion, they seemed to drink the most. It made me recall that during freshers' week Diane was waiting outside a room where they were holding a Sikh Society meeting waiting for some friends inside. She was invited to join the society. Now, she doesn't look Asian. Did they think she was Asian? We had therefore gone full circle now that we were partying with them. God, Diane must be sick of being mistaken for everything that she is not. I would be.

Diane and a fellow student, June, helped Nelson and Chika prepare for the party. Nelson and Chika were responsible for the music, Diane and June for the food. On the day of the party the food prepared was curried goat, rice, plantain and something called 'moi moi', which I had no idea what it was, although I now make it for Francis having been taught the recipe by his mother. Chika and Nelson visited the local Sony electrical store and asked to rent a music system for the weekend to try it out before buying it. They left a large deposit. The music system together with the speakers was covered in newspaper and plastic to preserve their cleanliness and prevent any damage or spillage. The system was used for the party and then promptly returned on Monday morning with a request that the deposit be returned to Nelson and Chika as the system was not as powerful as they had anticipated. *That's how you hire a system for a party*, I thought! The system was used for that weekend without any money being paid at all as the deposit was given back.

While at the party I noticed that Francis Egbo was standing in the corner, as per usual. He was very shy and appeared not to drink. He did not ask anyone to dance. He was doing his normal routine of just standing there and staring at me. Quite frankly, I was getting bored with it. Either he will make a move to talk to me – or anyone for that matter, the freak – or he will not. I certainly wasn't going to go over to talk to him first. I really should have stuck to my first impressions. I thought him snobbish, childish and arrogant – and he is, or certainly was at the time. I should have realised that if someone makes you mad, you really like them!

Following Nelson and Chika's party the Nigerian Society decided to throw a party themselves to match, which they thought would beat Chika and Nelson's. Quite innocently, Chika and Nelson invited Diane, June and me to their party. We turned up at the given address and as we walked through the front door we were met by a group of female Nigerian students who were dancing together. They took one look at us and just stood there and stared. It was really quite farcical. It was almost as if we had walked into a bar in a Western movie and the music had stopped. All three of us looked at each other and thought *what the hell have we done? Have we walked into something that we should not have done?* We made an about-turn on our heels and walked back out as we had come in. Chika and Nelson met us by the door, having witnessed the incident. They tried to keep us at the party, but we were adamant: we were uncomfortable and wanted to leave. Francis was in the corner and this was probably the first time he had actually said anything to me more than a hello. He apologised for the behaviour of his countrywomen who did not make us feel welcome and decided that he would accompany us to the local pub. We all sat down and got drunk together. The following morning I woke up with such a hangover it was painful and I was delirious. My mouth felt like someone had put sandpaper in it and my head was beginning to swirl as if someone was inside with a pneumatic drill. I thought I was going to throw up, but something told me this was not the first time I had that sensation within the last 12 hours. As I opened my eyes I realised I was not in my room. These were not my sheets. Where the hell was I? Oh shit, someone is in the bed with me. Oh shit, it's Francis f*****g Egbo! How the hell did that happen?

I can't tell you how we moved from the pub to his room except that I believe my drinks were spiked. I have no recollection. I remember standing up protesting that as a child of Irish parents I could drink any of them under the table and it seemed that the tables had turned on me. Especially when Chika and Nelson ordered some Nigerian Guinness that the pub had begun to stock as a result of the number of Nigerian students that asked for it. All I remember wondering was *what the hell was that?* It was nothing like Irish Guinness. As I was coming to, I remember thinking *I hope we used protection. Please don't make me pregnant. Please don't make me pregnant. Please don't make me pregnant.*

I crept out of the bed, dressed while Francis was still asleep and went back home. Diane and June were waiting for me and they had both agreed that if I hadn't returned home by 12 noon they were coming to get me. Chika and Nelson were sitting with them. I then had the third degree. Even Chika and Nelson were not impressed. I believed they may have wanted me for themselves and not share me with another Nigerian who they thought of as rude, unworthy and a little boy! I later learnt they were just being the protective friends I did not appreciate at the time.

I somehow managed to survive that Sunday without throwing up. I got increasingly anxious as I had to return to polytechnic on Monday, the next day. I wasn't sure what I could or should say to Francis and how he would greet me. His normal stance was to stand and stare, and I felt that our next meeting could or should be different. I turned up for the contract lecture early the next day without Diane, June, Nelson or Chika. I had hoped to speak with Francis directly. We did not have mobile phones in those days. We met each other outside the lecture hall and he just raised an eyebrow, said, "Good morning" and walked off. Nothing had changed then. I felt so angry with myself but I suppose that is the student life and what happens if you allow alcohol to take over your system! I vowed then never to sleep with another Nigerian in my life, and the only two Nigerian men I would talk to from then on were Chika and Nelson. I now looked at the Asian men on the course with new eyes. I wanted different and I was pissed off with Francis.

During the third term of our first year, Diane and I decided that Dudley was too far to travel daily and we moved to Whitmore Reams, Wolverhampton. We were walking up and down the streets where we knew students lived, looking for suitable accommodation. We could not find anywhere. I had returned to the Law Library to complete some work but Diane continued to search as if she was possessed. She wanted to find a property before it was too late. Diane came across a Sikh man, Mr Singh, speaking to his builders in Bright Street. She stopped him and asked whether he knew of anyone who was renting in the area, as she was desperate to find accommodation for four law students. Diane had deliberately said law students as she wanted to create an impression in this man's mind that they were students studying and not students who would be partying and would redecorate the house.

Mr Singh looked at her as if she had gone mad, but confirmed he was standing outside a property he had just purchased and was renovating for rental, and it would be ready the first week after Easter if she would be interested. She looked around and thought that it would be suitable as there were three bedrooms and two reception rooms downstairs separated by a wall. She felt it could hold four students who were looking for accommodation so she bartered and Mr Singh agreed that he would be happy to rent the place to four female law students. This was much better than the previous accommodation we had visited further down in Whitmore Reams: it had been cold and the walls were so full of damp that you could put a nail through the wall just by pressing it with your finger. Only God knows what diseases you could get!

When we all met up with Diane later in the library she told us of her find in great detail. We all went to see Mr Singh that evening and closed the deal. The only problem was there was no central heating but we soon learnt that central heating had not reached the Midlands and they felt those of us from the south were pampered and weak.

We now had a clean property to live in. Mr Singh and Diane kept in touch for a number of years after we left Wolverhampton as he had formed a very good relationship with Diane's stepfather. Whenever he came to pick Diane up at the end of each year to bring her home he would always end up in the pub with Mr Singh – usually a Sikh pub with Sikh men who shouldn't be drinking. Of the four of us, Mr Singh only allowed Diane to store possessions she did not wish to take home during the summer months in the basement of his home for free. Diane thought she got on well with Mr Singh but one day it was his wife who turned up to collect the rent. She could not speak a word of English but she could count money! Diane never warmed to her.

Next time Diane saw Mr Singh she asked him why his wife did not speak English and Mr Singh confirmed he did not want his wife to speak English, as to do so would allow her to converse with men of another religion or race. If she were able to converse freely there was every likelihood she could have an affair or someone could coerce her into action that she did not wish to take, and compromise herself. If she couldn't communicate in English with them, then she couldn't be coerced.

When Diane relayed the story to me, I thought this odd and noted this did not apply to their son, who often turned up at our rented home during the Easter and summer breaks with his Brummie and Wolverhampton girlfriends. But a blind eye was turned to it by his parents. I suppose the men could do what they pleased but the women could not. It is also nonsense to believe that just because we are separated by a language it means you are unable to feel the connection with another person.

At a party during our first year, this time held by a West Indian student, a very quiet African woman was found in the corner practically having sex with a White Midlander who was older, very clever and not the sort of individual you would have expected to behave that way in public, let alone with someone he never exchanged words with. Wolverhampton was strange and it did strange things to people. He spoke with an incomprehensible Black Country accent and she spoke with a heavy Nigerian accent. We were all wondering how the hell that worked. They could not speak to each other but still got on.

Whitmore Reams had a lot of shops which were owned by Asian businessmen and to get from the house to the Law Library we could go through a series of alleys which cut down the time it would take us. Once, as I was walking with Diane and June and we were late for class, we went through the alleyways and there were two little boys who were playing football with their mangy-looking dog. They didn't bat an eyelid at me but they turned on Diane and June. They called Diane a 'Paki'. Diane and I laughed to each other thinking it was hilarious but rather than do anything to frighten the boys, Diane looked at them, bent down and said, "If you're gonna insult me can you please do it properly, I'm not a Paki, I'm a nigger." The boys looked at each other with their mouths open as if swallowing air and ran off with their dog! Diane stood there laughing at them and the situation. In the 1980s, colour was so obvious but it meant nothing to Diane and me. I suppose she is right: if you are going to insult someone at least take the time to make sure that you know what you're talking about. It does make you look a bit stupid if you haven't got your facts straight before you start pontificating and insulting people!

During those years at Wolverhampton there was a lot of resistance from various communities. The Asian communities were separated between the Muslims, Hindus and Sikhs. The Black community between the Smallies and the Yardies and Africans, and the White community were just about thinking *what the hell is happening with our community*? It was a strange time racially and it seemed everyone was learning how to get on with each other. There was a lot of resistance from the settled Midlands community and a number of Black and ethnic minority students were attacked in the early hours of the morning by the subway. West Indians had only started coming to the UK in the 1950s and the Asians after that. We took to going out in groups and never allowing students to walk on their own. If they went home for the weekend and were travelling back from the train station, we were all insistent that we should use taxis to get from the station to the halls of residence or our various digs. None of us wanted to come face to face with the 'Subway Army' who attacked anyone and everyone not from Wolverhampton. They were indiscriminate. Their only criterion was that you were not White.

Diane returned home as often as she could as she missed her family, especially her sisters, Joanne and Nora-Jean.

Diane found a place that would stock Thunderbird wine and would always buy a bottle of Blue and Red Label to take home to her parents. We also found a very cheap market where she was able to buy clothes for Nora-Jean. She would always use 10 pence to call her mother just to say, "Hi, I am fine," speak for a few minutes and then cut off.

Anyway, back to the Subway Army. They were, as the name suggests, a group of young men who would roam the subways of Wolverhampton and the Birmingham New Road.

One evening, June, Diane and I went to a disco at the Students' Union. We decided at 12.30am to leave to wander back to Whitmore Reams. As we were walking down by the subway, we noticed that there was a group of men and boys behind us. The Subway Army always wore handkerchiefs over their faces as if they were cowboys. We thought they were more like coward boys and they obviously covered their faces so they wouldn't be recognised or arrested. We started to move faster and they started to move faster. In horror, their numbers started to swell. I don't know who was the first person to suggest that we needed to run to get away.

Diane had run for the London Borough of Merton while at Ursula Convent and was a fast sprinter. As she tried to get away, June, who was wearing heels, was trying to hold on to her to wait for her. Diane wasn't about to stop and told June she had better take off her shoes as we were clearly faced with trouble and we needed to run and run like we had stolen something! We all managed somehow to not get killed on the motorway that night as we were running like lunatics down the central reservation towards Bright Street and into Whitmore Reams.

As we turned the corner, there were several large houses with big front gardens and we darted into the first one we came to that was able to hide us from their view. We hid as the Army went past. I remember thinking that these houses in the Midlands were much bigger than they were in south

London. If you lifted up those houses and dropped them into Wimbledon Village they would be worth four times as much as they were worth in Wolverhampton. I then began to think what a stupid thing to think of after being chased by the Subway Army and running for your life! None of us breathed at this time and the exhilaration almost made us wet ourselves.

We thought that if we breathed louder than normal, the Subway Army would hear us and return and come back for us. I don't know how long we stayed there in those bushes but by the time we all stood up to walk back home, we could barely walk. We were overtaken by fear and our legs seemed to have turned to jelly. We somehow managed to make it back home. We all sat in the living room and looked at each other and burst into fits of giggles and then tears. We hadn't realised how much the situation had stressed us out. We were seconds away from being beaten, raped, killed or all three. We vowed that we would avoid the subway like the plague and walk the long way round in future. Hysteria can go one of two ways: you can either laugh or cry, the emotions are so close.

During the early years, we had spent a lot of time out and about, but we also tried to work hard as well. We didn't work as hard as we should have done, but we all still managed to get a 2:2 at the end of the year. Bearing in mind the amount of partying we did, it really should have been a third, but secretly we all wanted a 2:1 so were disappointed. Peer pressure is a dangerous thing. During the year you want to party and you believe that in the six weeks before the exams you can cram in everything you had or should have learnt during the year that you would need to pass an exam. Hundreds of thousands of students had done this in years gone by. You stayed up all night to revise. You slept during the day because of the noisy neighbourhood children going to and from school. You do enough to pass. Even now, at my age with four children, I still can't sleep until midnight and even if I am dog tired and I fall asleep on the sofa before I go upstairs to bed, I still don't sleep through the night. Those intense years of working through the night seem to have taken their toll on my sleeping habits that my body has never fully recovered from.

In later years when doing the night shift with the kids, this enforced insomnia would come in handy but it would mean my day was complete oblivion. When you have four kids sleep deprivation is a common occurrence and ain't no joke. The key thing from this period is that I can share with my children the need to go to university and work... but not all the time.

I know how difficult it was to sit down and revise and to have a structured day. I was able to help my children learn from my mistakes. I was bright enough for a 2:1 but ended up with a 2:2. In truth I chose going out and having fun over study. It is only three years out of your life but if you don't put in the time then it can affect you in later years, as we all learnt to our peril. You may never catch up. Most City law firms would only take students with a 2:1 or above and for those with grades below we were either relegated to Legal Aid firms or high street or medium-sized firms.

However, we ended up in the City anyway when Diane opened her firm. Diane's view was that her career was a bit like a football match: if you couldn't strike for goal at the first opportunity then you should kick the ball back to the halfway line and start again from a different direction. I suppose we are all like fine wines and improve with age!

At the end of each year at Wolverhampton the law students always completed their exams first, which meant that we were revising while our friends on the other courses – accounts, humanities etc. – were still partying as they did not have to get their heads down for a few weeks. By the time we finished, they were smack-bang in the middle of exams and revision so the law students would leave early and return to their various parts of the world.

Diane and I were travelling to Euston station and June agreed to travel with us as she was going to see her sister who lived at Elephant and Castle. I hadn't spoken to him for months but Francis was sitting in the corner seat on the train, as per usual on his own with his head in a book. I had had enough of this nonsense and his coldness. We had slept together, big deal, he needed to get over it – or did I? I decided to sit opposite him whilst June and Diane sat elsewhere. He had no option but to talk to me and we had our first proper conversation in those few hours. We never spoke about that night. He took my number in London and promised that he would call me during the summer break and I thought that yes, of course he would.

I had secretly warmed to him over the past few months and I could not understand why he was being such a prat. Maybe that was why I warmed to him – he ignored me and it annoyed me. It annoyed me and I wanted to get the better of the situation. I now know that he was very shy and not only was I his first sexual partner, he was also in conflict with himself as to whether he should continue with such a relationship that his father would view as taboo. He as the youngest of 20 children – yes 20, and the child of his father's fourth wife. He wanted to make a name for himself and thought the easier option was to keep his head down and study, as his father was paying a lot of money for his education as an overseas student.

I understood more about him in those hours on that train journey to London than I did in the 10 months on the first year of our course. We parted company at Euston station with me hoping that he would call but trying to be blasé about it on the outside. It was a pleasant surprise therefore when, several days later, he did call and left a message for me with my mother. She knew my father and his dislike of Africans and kept the call a secret. It was weird, as I don't think Francis had an accent, but maybe he did and I just got used to it. Thank God it was my mother who answered the phone and not anyone else in my house. I agreed that I would call Francis next time, and we agreed a time and I would go to the telephone box and call away from my family. We took it in turns to call, but never met up as we knew that by September or October we would be back together again in Wolverhampton for the last two years of the course.

During that summer I signed on to receive the dole to my father's horror. I wasn't working. I was tired and needed a rest. I didn't want to get a job. I took everything very seriously. My relationship with Francis grew into a friendship and then much later to lovers, but we both knew we needed to keep our heads down and pass the course, at least for Francis's sake. He was petrified of his father and the thought of failure really made him quite unwell.

We managed somehow to get through the next two years with our sanity intact and our little group ended up with 2:2s. Francis got a 2:1, bastard! We had decided to do the solicitors' finals course in London and June went off to Chester. Diane, Francis and I went to Breams Building off Chancery Lane, London.

Our time at Chancery Lane was strange, although we made some very good lifelong friends. It was still the 1980s. Francis, Diane and I continued where we left off in Wolverhampton and worked hard, played hard, but somehow looked after each other. We were always invited to parties but didn't always attend – we were all becoming quite square either because we were getting older or we just were too tired from all the work we had on the Law Society finals course. The course was really taking its toll on us all and by the end of the year you had several A4 folders of information to get into your brain in order to pass the course.

We all had to look for articles (now called training contracts) that year. I was offered a training contract at Ellis Solicitors and Diane and Francis were without training contracts. I know they were as good as me academically and I can only assume it was sheer prejudice that prevented them from getting training contracts. All of the minorities, including Black people and Asians, on the course were without training contracts that year. Every single one! Diane and Francis continued to look for a training contract to be admitted to the Roll of Solicitors. I knew I was going to be looking for a hospital bed and being admitted to the maternity ward with my first child. Wahala!

CHAPTER 4

Sly and the Family Stone

LAW REPORTS

LAW REVIEW

CIVIL LAW

LEGAL DICTIONARY

I love my life. I am now employed by my best friend after years of working for megalomaniacs in large, medium, small, City and high street practices. Let me tell you they are all the same, solicitors. The urgency of work and the threat of complaints make them too stressed and they burn out.

I am married to the man I love and have loved for years. I have four great children and I am smug. But my mind keeps telling me it is too good and something must go wrong. I try to put that voice out of my head but it won't budge. I wonder what it could be that is making me so uneasy…

It's Friday night and Baby Boy is in bed. Hip hip hooray! No dramas tonight. He had his wash and went straight to bed. That in itself is a cause for celebration. The other three are out because… well it's Friday night! Right! It's just Francis and me alone in the house with Baby Boy tucked up upstairs in bed. Having four children leaves us too tired for romance or anything else for that matter but we do still like our music. We tune into Choice FM and Sly and the Family Stone – *Everyday People* – is being played.

Listening to the radio, we are both giving it a bit of welly in the kitchen as it is one of our favourite songs. It takes me back to the early 1980s when Diane and I used to go to the Walton Hop at Walton-on-Thames with our school friends. We used to sneak out and pretend that we were all at McDonalds in Wimbledon. We had to rush back home from Walton to Wimbledon on the last bus otherwise our parents would ground us if we were late. They never caught on to this which makes me smile. If they did, they never let on. We always made sure we were home at the agreed time.

Francis and I are singing along:

> *"Sometimes I am right and I can be wrong*
>
> *My own beliefs are in my song*
>
> *The butcher, the banker, the drummer and then mix*
>
> *Makes no difference what group I'm in."*

I think as I hear these words how funny it is that another song called *Everyday People* was later sung by Arrested Development and that nothing really is original. Although this version is quite something:

> *"The butcher, the banker…"*

What were they thinking? Bankers these days are viewed as the lowest of the low because of the mess that they have left this country in. For reasons best known to me and my God, as I am dancing in my kitchen, I think of a book I read years ago called *Meltdown*. That man got the mood right!

Humph, I sigh. The bankers, and their risky selves, caused the current trouble in the first place. All the trouble and strife that we are suffering from was at their hands but are their bonuses cut? Not a chance. Francis just lost his job again. He is a litigator by training and there is little cash in his field. He does not have the banker's bonuses and with all the 'No Win No Fee' Agreements (Conditional

Fee Agreements) and After the Event insurance flooding into the legal market, clients don't pay monthly bills like they used to. Litigation funding has changed drastically. The insurance market for funding now affects cash flow and firms can't afford to pay their way and are probably trading insolvently. You need to have enough live cases that end in regular month cycles so by the time you get the file taxed and paid, payment will be monthly or every other month, thereby helping cash flow. He came in last, he went out first.

"There is a blue one who can't accept the green one

For living with the fat one trying to be the skinny one

And different strokes for different folks and so on and so on and Scooby dooby doo – bee

Different strokes for different folks."

Oh my God! What made me think of that little man from *Different Strokes* and the trouble he got into? I don't quite understand children reaching such popularity so early in life. Look at Michael Jackson. Seriously weird!

Scooby Doo makes me smile but for different reasons. It is my favourite cartoon. I love to watch *Scooby Doo* and *Tom and Jerry* on a Saturday morning. It is helpful having kids because you can pretend you are watching cartoons with them when I enjoy it more than they do. As the older kids have lost interest as they got older I am trying to introduce Baby Boy into the world of cartoons but he is not having it. He likes real people, real faces, and real life.

Life has now taken over and I do not have any Saturday mornings to myself. Saturdays involve ferrying Jack and the grandkids around. Oh yeah, just in case life isn't interesting enough, Francis Junior has decided he wants to start his family very early! It would have helped if he did not follow the family tradition of children first then marriage after! He has a one-year-old that I look after for him every third weekend of the month. The mother is OK but she and Francis are not together. I am proud he does try to look after his son.

My mother-in-law helps out also and lives in Oxfordshire. She is nice enough but a bit of a fruitcake fighting over her boys – any boys: sons, grandsons, nephews etc. I think it is a cultural thing.

Crikey, as we are singing and dancing I begin to think *what is the point?* No really, what the hell is the point? The whole world is becoming brown and what was the reason behind this song in the first place? My family is Everyday People living in one household.

> *"We've got to live together."*
>
> *"I am no better and neither are you*
>
> *We are the same whatever we do*
>
> *You love me you hate me you know me and then*
>
> *You can't figure the bag I'm in."*

I don't even know what bag I'm in these days. I am White Irish, Francis is Black African, and my dad is Catholic.

My mother is a tinker and an even more devout Catholic than Dad. Francis's father is a Chief in Nigeria and they are Catholic. What is the difference? In the 60s when Dad first came to the UK he was living in this melting pot and together the lines seemed to have blurred somewhat from then on. I grew up listening to ska, reggae beats and have more in common with the Black community than the White. With the introduction of the Mods and Rockers confrontation, the battle lines were drawn and everything started to get blurred. It wasn't uncommon for different racial groups to intermarry but they got grief. There is an increase in Black/White relationships but little Asian/White/Black – in fact there were very few Asians with anyone other than Asians perhaps with the exception of Caribbean Asians. What the hell bag were they in and why is it so important today?

> *"There is a long hair that doesn't like the short hair for bein' such a rich one that will not help the poor one!"*

Ain't that a bitch? We now have to work hard to look after the family, and with the cost of living so high how do poor people cope?

> *"There is a yellow one that won't accept the black one*
>
> *That won't accept the red one that won't accept the white one."*

Age ain't nothing but a number and colour ain't nothing but a label to discriminate.

As I am still laughing at the significance of the song *Everyday People* today, you would not believe the next song on the radio for the love of the Crucified Saviour! Do you believe in coincidences? *We Are Family* by Sister Sledge. Diane and I used to sing this song at the Walton Hop.

Francis and I are brought back to reality as Baby Boy comes into the kitchen with his wet PJs and asks for yet another glass of water. I have explained to him, if I have explained a hundred times, that he cannot have anything to eat or drink after 7 o'clock at night. I stand there negotiating with a five-year-old – what a life but we are a family.

We negotiate throughout our lives. When Francis and I qualified, we had the big negotiation of power in our 'professional household' and how was the choice made that I would stay at home and Francis go out to work? Simple, he is African and in his culture men provide for their women.

I have friends and colleagues who have found the experience of child rearing quite traumatic. Gillian was someone I met at the Law Society. Her partner supported her throughout their respective training contracts – or articles as they were then called. She was at a much larger City firm than him and on a very good salary and prospects. Upon qualification she became pregnant fairly quickly. With her City training she was always going to be in a better position than him to secure a more lucrative salary for their family; however, he was no longer supportive once she gave birth to 'his' son. The negotiation of power in that household was quite clearly strained.

Gillian became an assistant in a mid-sized firm as she could no longer work the hours required of the 'magic circle' City firms, which expected her to give her blood, sweat, tears and more. Her husband did eventually get into the City. With the introduction of more and more women into the legal profession, it appeared some firms viewed men as a novelty in that there weren't that many. The numbers of men coming through were shrinking. Gillian's husband progressed quite quickly throughout his career in the City and has never looked back – until he had an affair that is! Gillian was distraught over the affair and the couple packed up and moved south to Devon to be with her parents. He had to give up his relationship with the City law firms and his mistress!

It is a shame that if he wasn't such a prick, Gillian would have had quite a good life but she never negotiated what they would do post-children and what they would have done in their careers BEFORE they got married. It came as a shock when Gillian was told she would have to stay at home to look after the child but it also gave her husband an excuse to look elsewhere!

But we don't think about that when we go into a relationship. You really need to ask yourself, "Is this who I want to have my kids with?" We think it will be forever and we don't think too deeply on the problems that could emerge if anything goes wrong. Everyone performs well when things are going right. But how do they perform when things are going badly? Francis and I sort of had that discussion at the beginning of our relationship but it was never an issue for us; everything to him was 'wahala' and he sees everything as trouble, suffering and a big problem but resolvable.

Notwithstanding our trials and tribulations, we are everyday people in one family and my life reflects that of Diane my best friend, colleague and confidante:

a) We both have immigrant parents, (Ireland/Caribbean) who come from very different backgrounds. As the first generation of migrant parents who wanted us to do better than they did, they instilled in us a work ethic that home-grown Brits did not seem to have.

b) We both have two sisters, two brothers.

c) We were both the middle children, three out of five, and had to fight for the attention. We were not the eldest and we were not the youngest but we wanted to be heard and still had something to say.

d) We both believe in the power of family.

e) We are both Cancerians through and through!

f) We are both clinically mad.

g) We both simultaneously love our siblings and family and hate them at the same time! But I suppose hurt people hurt others but we're the hardest on the people that we love the most. We do need to break some cycles: certain family traits keep repeating themselves especially sibling rivalry. Mum never really got on with her brothers and sisters nor the travelling community in Ireland which is why she came to the UK. I don't get on with all of my siblings as well as I would like. Mum and I are very similar in that respect.

I am closer to my mum in height and looks but I have my dad's outgoing temperament. My mum is a mystery to me and I find it difficult that she can somehow be so distant with her family but helpful to others. She can sometimes appear detached but has great insight into my friends' lives and helps them when they come over and they all think she is wonderful. See me, come live with me are two very different things. She has these spiritual evenings where she reads tarot cards, stones and palms and is genuinely upset by the time the session is finished because it drains her emotionally, mentally and physically. I find myself asking the question *why can't she put that amount of attention into her family?* Mum and Dad grew apart years ago and I suppose the difference in their backgrounds just couldn't be bridged. As they are both devout Catholics, they stayed together and never dreamed of divorce as Diane's parents had done. Dad ended up where he ran away from in the first place which was a pub. Mum now fancies herself as an Irish Mystic Meg.

I have always believed in spiritualism and the power of the spirit (holy and otherwise!). Dreams are important and the power of the mind equally so, but Mum would never explain it to me. I have had my cards read but not by her. It was a revelation as I was told that I was one of six and it was explained to me the first child looked like Dad, the second looked like Mum, the third would look like Mum and the fourth would look like both. I said that I look like both but I am the third. I was told I was not the middle child and in actual fact I look like both parents and was the fourth.

I protested but when I went home and mentioned it to Mum she went a very serious shade of grey. She confided in me that that was the reason she had left Ireland all those years ago and that she had become pregnant by a young man from the settled Irish community and she had to be sent to England because of the shame. She did not carry the child to full-term but I suppose the medium had picked up that in actual fact that was her first child so to speak. It was our secret and I have never revealed this to any other member of my family, least of all Dad. I was also told that America would be a focal point in my life! But I have never been there and we have no intention of going. I wondered then as I do now how America would fit into my plans. Maybe I have Irish/American ancestry. Wahala – again. I say this a lot!

CHAPTER 5

Junior Lawyer: 1988 – 1998

I was successful in securing a training contract at Ellis Solicitors. I hid my pregnancy well. Both Diane and Francis went for interviews at many City law firms. Francis was rejected, we think, by virtue of his name. Diane, however, secured many interviews as her name was not necessarily ethnic sounding and so, as a result, she was selected for interviews. Upon attending the interviews she was never successful. It became a very boring tedious journey. It may very well be she was not good enough but there was a voice in the back of her mind suggesting it was because of her ethnicity as her grades were as good as anyone else's that I knew who was obtaining training contracts at that time. Was law institutionally racist? I think for a long time interviewers used themselves as yardsticks so they picked people who looked, sounded and acted like them. This isn't necessarily racist; they are just picking what they are comfortable with as anything else was relatively 'unknown'.

It was several weeks after the end of the Law Society finals course when Diane announced that she was woken up by her mother with the arrival of the first post. In those days you had a first class and second class delivery. Not so much now – you are lucky if you get one delivery per day.

There was a letter stamped with Hurst & Co's name on it. Who knew they would be her new employers? Diane likes to recount the story that when she first travelled to their offices she was in mixed minds whether to accept the job as, like everyone else, she had bitten the City bug and wanted to obtain a training contract in a City firm. I am not so sure she would have coped with the City or indeed whether they would have coped with her! Hindsight is a wonderful thing but it is, after all, hindsight. Diane had passed her driving test very early in her 20s and so was driving a Mini Metro which we all lovingly referred to as BB because it was the colour of a bumblebee. She was invited for an interview at Hurst & Co's regional office which was on Haydons Road, Wimbledon where we both used to live – how spooky! She sat in BB and looked at the offices across the road.

It was almost as if she had gone full circle as she now lived in Surrey with her parents but they had moved from Wimbledon in 1984. Diane was very relaxed. She appeared to get on well with the senior partner, Mr Hurst, who was interviewing her. He offered her his cigarettes during the interview which she took and smoked. This was the job she did not really want as she was a snob and wanted the City but she was offered a training contract by that firm and these are the same people that have helped her through her articles, as a junior solicitor, a young partner and then later when she opened her own firm.

Diane was not overenthusiastic about taking the position at Hurst & Co because she stupidly thought her place was in the City and she wanted to work in the City with her friends. She realised, however, that she needed to seize every opportunity that came her way. She needed to listen and answer any questions. She needed to leave a footprint. She had the echoes of the convent in her ears in that as a member of an ethnic group was she setting her standards too high?

She decided that she would accept the training contract at Hurst & Co even though it was not 100% what she wanted, but what she didn't know was that it was *exactly* what she needed.

Diane, June and I had a reunion in Wimbledon. We sat one evening in the Crooked Billet public house in Wimbledon Village – the very same pub Dad had been taken to all those years ago by the Tree Trunks and then moved on to the Hand in Hand next door. We spoke about our early years, Wolverhampton, training contracts. Basically, how we came to where we were today. We also spoke about our school and the standards that we set for ourselves. Diane reluctantly accepted she did not fit the mould of what the City required even though she wanted to be there. Diane was rejected by the City firms but it is bizarre that 18 years later and after post-qualification, she was back in the City where she was rejected in the first instance – but as a business owner.

The legal profession in the 1990s operated a revolving door practice. You went into the system as a member of an ethnic group and you thought you had made it to the other side, but actually the door was still revolving and you were on your way out before you were on your way in! In watching Diane and Francis I am not sure the door in fact was revolving. It more resembled a trap door! Francis did not have a training contract for some time after Diane but he persevered. Diane and I used to give him mock interviews and he was always interviewed but not successful in obtaining a job.

Accepting the training contract at Hurst & Co was one of best things that Diane could have done with her career. Her training principal was a young man from Oxford University and a nice man. Diane often recounts the story that she had offered him a Murray Mint. Yes, a sweet! When she looked up he had changed to a peculiar shade of red. When she asked what was the matter, he said, "What did you say?" She confirmed, "I offered you a Murray Mint." He replied, "Thank God for that, I thought you had offered to marry me and I was about to say yes!" Diane thought this amusing but since those days in 1988 she has remained firm friends with Hurst & Co and with the partners who are unaware of the ways in which they have assisted her.

Mr Hurst was the senior partner at Hurst & Co. He was everything that Diane should object to on principle. He was sexist, he was a bigot, and could be quite nasty but Diane was able to see through his behaviour and demeanour.

There was a time when Mr Hurst had hurt his hip and Diane went to see him in hospital. He was talking to a colleague who had asked Diane where she was born. Diane confirmed that she was a very reasonable individual and that she was born in Clapham but not on a bus. Mr Hurst said under his breath, "Oh I thought it was Brixton." Diane let it pass as she was sure that if he tried that nonsense with her again she would deal with him but away from other individuals. She let him have that moment.

As a trainee at Hurst & Co she came across many obstacles which she would often recount to me. She was still so enthusiastic. I was jealous of her life as I could only talk about raising kids. Her life seemed so much more interesting, even more interesting than Francis's who after many months of trying had secured a training contract with a local authority and got the job as a housing litigator. At this time I was opening nappy bags. Diane was opening new client files. It was a long time before she got her first PA, Rita, who was formerly with the military police. She advised Diane to "put the Dictaphone in front of your mouth, lose the food and dictate with the phonetic alphabet!"

This has stayed with Diane until today so when I eventually became her own PA she had dictation down to a T and I too had to learn the phonetic alphabet. I was spelling something to Diane once in a pub. We were overheard by the people at the table next to us who looked at us with horror. They asked if we were police officers – nope, not that side of the law!

Just before Diane qualified she told us how she was asked by Mr Hurst as well as all the other partners to attend a fee earners' meeting and to provide her view on where she thought the firm was going. Each fee earner was given a different topic on which to prepare a paper.

Diane assumed that this was a genuine request and that she should speak freely. Why wouldn't it be? Her response was based on what she saw and what she felt. She felt the firm was triangular in shape: Mr Hurst was at the top and the partners next down. The assistants were then closely followed by members of staff, forming a triangle. She felt this was not healthy and not the way to run a firm and unhealthy for progression, and that a firm needed to grow organically and externally. She felt that because all of the partners had formerly been employees and trainees of Mr Hurst himself, they would be in a difficult position to question his authority. If they were like Mr Hurst they would leave to open their own firms because they were entrepreneurs. If they stayed, it may be because they felt it was safe. It is very difficult to work out how to nurture individuals who are similar to you and maybe the offer of a partnership is/was the end. If your staff were like you then they would leave to open their own firm, and how do you keep them without damaging your practice?

Diane had sent in her paper and hoped it was clear. The paper was drafted in manuscript. She did not have full typing facilities at that time. Although she had access to Rita, Rita was shared with a partner and she would often do the partner's work before Diane's. I had read her paper before she submitted it and offered to type it up. But she said no. She let me read it but felt it would be better received in manuscript as it would highlight the point that she was not given full resources. I knew exactly what was in it as I had read it and even I thought she was a little bit too honest! But Diane knows best!

Before the fee earners' meeting, Mr Hurst confirmed he did not wish to view any responses apart from Diane's. Diane felt that that was her warning card and she needed to clear her desk and go home as she was going to lose her job and that was the end of her legal career. The papers prepared by the other solicitors were circulated prior to the meeting. The other partners had somehow managed to frighten Diane into thinking that her document was a little too risqué. It was all in her head.

The meeting went without incident and Mr Hurst seemed OK. The expected explosion did not happen. After the meeting, he invited Diane to the local pub, the Blue Dragon, and confirmed to her that in all his years of practice, Diane was the only person who said what he did not wish to hear and he was very thankful for her honesty. It was unlikely he would implement the changes she had suggested in his practice in her paper but at least he acknowledged that she made a point in some instances.

She and Mr Hurst have remained friends and at his 75th birthday party there were only two partners from his several decades of practice in law: Diane and one partner from Hurst.

Although in many respects Mr Hurst was a questionable individual in Diane's eyes, like me Diane realised that you should see through the façade of people and look at the individual underneath. He may have been many things that were abhorrent to most people but he did teach Diane how to run a firm and she used a lot of his principles when she opened her own practice several years later. Between the two of us, running a practice would be child's play.

Diane enjoyed her time at Hurst & Co and had the opportunity to work in their Wimbledon and later City offices. I was working part-time at that time as a legal secretary while Francis Junior was at nursery. I had experienced enough of changing nappies, different types of processed foods and daytime TV and needed to get out and speak to adults during the day.

Diane began to question whether she should move on to pastures new. She did not want to ask for partnership at Hurst & Co as she thought if she was good enough, it would be offered to her. After a few years it was. We celebrated together and she had a meeting with Mr Hurst which lasted several hours until he put his hands up in the air and said, "Enough!" Diane was asking too many questions surrounding her potential exposure and liability. She became a partner on paper only really and shared in a very small percentage of the profits. She also shared a very small percentage of the losses. The fact is she could be called and held as a partner on the letterhead which in her late 20s at the time was astonishing. I was very proud of her but she was not overly ecstatic. She thought *what was so exceptional?* She was a lawyer, female and Black – so what? As far as she was concerned she deserved it.

We kept in regular contact and met in Wimbledon Village with other former school members from the convent and Wandle High. We kept ourselves updated with what each other was doing. I was very jealous of their lives because I had very little to look forward to apart from part-time work and children whereas they recounted stories of their lives: Diane as a trainee/junior lawyer; Marcia was a lecturer at Kingston University and the craziness of the students; and Nikki a City lawyer.

As a trainee I learnt through Diane, Nikki and experience, you come across amazing stories which just bemuse you and teach you how to deal with life and not just the profession. You need to cut your teeth somewhere. Bad experiences can change your pathway as you look for easier areas of law to practice. Some of the early Legal Aid family cases Diane dealt with made her realise she had to change direction and fast.

On one occasion Diane had to go to court with a client who was fighting an application in a matrimonial case and where there was an allegation of him molesting his stepdaughter. He felt that his stepdaughter was not a member of his blood family and therefore she was not really family, but he did not touch her anyway, or so he said. Diane was disgusted. At court this client's wife cursed him for being a Muslim. I am not sure why this was suddenly relevant as he was Muslim when she married him! She even argued that he had turned up to court with a Muslim solicitor. Diane put her hands up in the air and said, "Sorry I am not a Muslim, I am Catholic!" Although the story is mildly amusing in that Diane was mistaken for another religion, the case also had a hint of alleged child molestation which made Diane uncomfortable.

Diane needed to get away from cases like this. As a Legal Aid family lawyer, she had to deal with behaviour at a level that perhaps others did/could not even think about/dream up.

She was sitting in her office one day when a client came in who wanted to get divorced. She explained that there was one ground but it could be proved by several facts and she went through the list: adultery, unreasonable behaviour, desertion, two years separation with consent, five years without. The client confirmed it was most definitely five years separation without consent. He was adamant. Diane then took down his details and asked the client where his wife resided. He confirmed the address as a local cemetery. It transpired his wife had passed away; he was very lonely and just wanted someone to talk to. It exasperated Diane because of the ever increasing mental health issues and care in the community which appeared not to work. In this case the client was completely harmless but clearly in need of human contact on a daily basis as he lived alone. It was pitiful and Diane soon grew to hate cases like this where they pulled on your heart strings!

In those days Legal Aid solicitors could make a good living. Diane and I had a mutual older colleague from college who had opened a Legal Aid practice. He was able to purchase a boat which he called the *Jolly Roger Street* because Legal Aid payments were then made through Roger Street and he named the boat in honour of the office that paid him. You could make a good living as they proved. Now Legal Aid is going south and will probably soon be called the Public Defender's Office!

Members of the public will always think and say that lawyers (in general) were fat cats. At one end we deal with lonely pensioners, at the other the system was such you could make a good living if you turned over enough work. The majority of lawyers in general are not fat cats. They give a good public service. They don't all have the opportunity to wear brogue shoes and designer suits. Some deal with the underprivileged in society and deal with them to the best of their legal ability. If Legal Aid goes, who will represent these people? Politicians and individuals in positions of power should recognise the need to support the public at this level as lawyers are the funnel through which their clients have access to justice. If that funnel is closed off, there is no access and therefore no justice for a large proportion of the population.

Diane eventually moved from the Wimbledon office of Hurst & Co to the West End office which was very close to Sussex Gardens. She was horrified that many of the hotels on Sussex Gardens were owned by wealthy businessmen. Diane loved the story of being mistaken for a 'working girl' one evening. As she was leaving the office quite late, carrying her briefcase, she was stopped by a 'punter' looking for an address and asked whether or not she was available! She confirmed that her briefcase contained papers only and no whips or other devices! She promptly sent him on his way. At the other end of Diane's practice she had very wealthy property developers. I don't know how she kept up with them but variety is the spice of life, I suppose.

It was interesting times at Hurst & Co but five years later Diane decided she was going to move on. She didn't make the decision because she disliked the practice or the people she worked with. She loved them all very much in their individual ways, but she left because she wanted more for herself. She felt she was in a rut, I know how she felt. She believed she had more to give and could not give any more at Hurst & Co. She wanted to spread her wings.

She still talks to the partners of Hurst & Co as she has a strong link with them. She qualified at that practice. Indeed her first case as a qualified lawyer was a motor accident claim for damages for the senior partner's son. He was driving his father's automatic BMW and the car careered into a wall off a roundabout. Diane was asked to represent him at Kingston upon Thames County Court. I remember she did not sleep for a week. It was a hilarious time for us to watch a control freak disintegrate right in front of our eyes, but horrendous for her.

At this time in the early 1990s the rights of audience for solicitors was confined mainly to the Lower Courts. Solicitors are now able to progress further and apply for higher rights of audience and the disparity between barristers and solicitors *may* eventually merge.

On the day of the hearing, Diane appeared at Kingston upon Thames County Court to be met by a qualified barrister. That made her dry up even more. I went with her for the hearing to give her moral support. It was amusing but also a very proud moment. I did feel her pain! From the time she stood up to present her case you could see she was nervous. If she had been asked to confirm her name she would not have been able to say it. The entire episode confirmed to her that she must always deal with what Mr Hurst called the six Ps: Proper Preparation Prevents Piss Poor Performance.

We have both tried to adopt this principle throughout our working careers and it has worked. When she finished the case the courtroom was full of barristers who had smiles on their faces, either because they thought *God help us if solicitors do advocacy* or they were just impressed with what they had seen, or laughing as a fellow barrister lost to a solicitor! Who cares? Diane had won her first case.

It was during her time at Hurst & Co that she came across the Society of Black Lawyers and managed to convince Francis to become involved as well. She felt it might help him move into private practice. She also joined the Association of Women Solicitors. She believed that the legal profession was suffering from PMS (pale, male and stale) and needed some oestrogen to neutralise the testosterone. She had to decide which was more important: her ethnicity or her gender. Both were equally important, but as a Black woman she could promote both in the Association of Women Solicitors. She will always be grateful to Hurst & Co for their support in training her and allowing her to go out and spread her wings. Many things happened during her career at that firm that she would take into practice at a later stage, not least of which how to run a practice effectively.

About that time and towards the end of her employment at Hurst & Co, Diane had met with her soon to become business partner in the summer of 1998 in Victoria, London. They had met with five or six others and agreed that they would hand in their respective notices. Some had to give six months' notice, she had to give three. The day she handed in her notice she placed it in the post for Mr Hurst. He did not see it immediately but when he did he called her in at approximately 11 o'clock. He confirmed he wanted to speak with her but not in the office and wanted to take her out to a pub. They arrived at the pub at 12 o'clock. It was the only pub in the area that was open to serve food at that time. They sat in the pub and Diane thinks they may have moved to a restaurant, she cannot be sure, until late that evening. During that time Mr Hurst confirmed that he had taken Hurst & Co to a level where he could not take it any further. He would have been disappointed if Diane had remained there all of her career and he accepted she needed to spread her wings and wished her well.

I think it is fair to say that Diane was the definition of blind drunk that evening. She got back to the office and fell up the stairs, if that is physically possible as most people fall down them. She then opened her office and fell into the room and into her filing cabinet, knocking over milk as she went. She had to call a friend – it was clearly not *Who Wants to be a Millionaire*! She called Francis and me. We went up to the office to get her and take her home. She was incapable of speaking and her then trainee had to dial our numbers for her as she couldn't see the phone numbers herself. She relayed Diane's behaviour on returning to the office. Diane was not allowed to speak to clients, which was fine as she couldn't speak anyway. She had taken the plunge and I looked at her in awe. She was either brilliant or mad but Francis said that as she had no children she could please herself. I think he was a little jealous of her ability to choose.

The following day Diane went paintballing with her sister-in-law and me. She decided she would be a sniper and hide out in the bushes but used it as an excuse to sleep for most of the day to try and sober up. She was hungover, felt sick and was trying not to throw up. However, she was relieved she had handed in her notice.

She thought the paintballing event would be a good opportunity for the tongues to wag at Hurst & Co for a day while she was away. On her return, everyone said how sad it was to see her go but at least they had had a day to get over the shock.

I also met with Diane the evening after the paintballing and she was very remorseful that she had to leave Hurst & Co. She felt as if they were her family. They had taught her a lot. Even though she had had her scraps with Mr Hurst, she had no real issues or concerns with the firm or him. It was what it was. She felt she could achieve more and wanted to for herself. She had made the decision that she was going to make or break and open her own firm.

Too many small things had happened at Hurst & Co where she felt it was now water under the bridge. The small things added together and made a slightly uncomfortable situation. She had met some wonderful people and she had learnt a lot. She remembers Mr Hurst asking the Law Society to come in and check his procedures. Most firms ran away from them. He was so sure of his compliance, he ran towards them. She took the latter into her practice and she also took some positive steps from the negative situations that had occurred.

Hurst & Co had a franchise with a drinks company in Middlesex. She worked all evening on their files until 10pm and weekends while the partner she sat with was away for two months. On one weekend Mr Hurst came in and confirmed to her that he was very impressed that she was working overtime but she would not receive any overtime pay and her reward would be "in heaven." She did not feel the comment was appropriate even in jest. She remembered that day, that as a junior lawyer you have to put in the hours that you need to put in and then, as now, the clients only call the shots. You have the Rules of Professional Conduct that you have to abide by and if you don't you'll get sued. Lawyers have to be 100%, 100% of the time and if you don't there's a claim on your indemnity.

She will never forget the time spent at Hurst & Co and the stories, and the efforts that were made to ensure that she became a rounded lawyer. If she had not had that experience she would not have entered into her second phase which was to open her own firm. Thank God she did not get a training contract in the City as I don't think that direction would have suited her at all and vice versa. The City would probably have demoralised her and she would have left the profession.

Francis and I helped her in conducting the research to setting up the new practice. We bought all the books on the market and prepared spreadsheets on the steps to be taken to open a firm as required by the Law Society. It was very easy to get started. These days you have to go through the Solicitors Regulation Authority and wait until your application is processed which can take several months.

We all trawled the market carefully for the best indemnity insurance for business start-ups and obtained a competitive rate. We looked at her client list from Hurst & Co and interrogated it. We worked out the type of clients that she worked with and the areas that we could help her market. We then put the clients into different categories and into a traffic light system: green for hot leads, amber for medium and red for cold but could be converted. We also assisted in drafting business models and plans for the bank in case she required finance. However, she decided she would open the firm with no overdraft and use her own private funds for the first six months so that she would not draw from the business as it was trying to grow.

Finance was the biggest area to look at. As a PA I loved spreadsheets as well as a non practising lawyer (in that I had completed the solicitor's finals but not my articles/ training contract); I understood the legal side of the business as well as the practical side, being part of the administrative support team. I helped work out what the practice had to bill to cover all costs, how many staff she needed to employ. Diane decided no staff in the first six months as she did not want to pay salaries which would add to the overall cost and reduce overall profit.

Francis was energised during this period as he secretly hoped she would invite him to join the practice; however, she was quite clear she could not. His area of work at the time was local authority housing and there was no place in a commercial practice in the City at that time. He would not be able to take his local authority work with him anyway as they needed teams in law firms to provide the service effectively and so he was in a difficult situation. Local authorities only instructed certain firms at that time.

He wanted to move from his current position in the local authority to private practice and we know Diane would have helped him if she could but we all had to be realistic. His current practice was just not going to fit in with her new business model.

We spent many days with Diane and her new business partner. They were evenly balanced which made me think of the relationship between men and women in the household, which is not as complicated as people think. It was reflected in the early days at the firm and its partners. Society can view men as the problem for diversity. Women are viewed as having problems. If it wasn't for Neanderthal men, women would have equality, but is this right? Women view equality as equal time that they put into a practice or the home and so are entitled to equal pay and equal consideration. Men view it slightly differently especially in a household, as who is contributing the most financially? Francis is a man. He provides for his family regardless of my earning capacity so end of conversation. The reality was with an expanded family we needed money.

Within the work setting, Diane settled on growing the practice organically by setting up the procedures whilst her business partner was more suited to matters such as marketing. It was a good match.

Francis and I are also a good match and I knew just how I was going to convince him so I could go back to full-time work. I would speak with his mother! His mother had always been a very calming influence on him. Although he can be sexist in many respects, he loves his mother and that is what I find fascinating. He will also do as she says – sometimes to my annoyance and against my wishes. He will do as he is told even at his age! It is frightening the amount of respect, or fear, he has for his mother. By the time he agreed to me returning to working full-time, Francis believed that he had thought of the idea of me working full-time in the first place! I got what I wanted and he got what he wanted, which was not to concede. His mum also got what she wanted. She had decided to move to the UK to look after her grandsons. She therefore took care of Francis Senior, Junior and Fiachra and within months my boys were speaking a dialect I couldn't understand.

CHAPTER 6

Change

"If you don't like something, change it.
If you can't change it, change your
attitude towards it."

Maya Angelou RIP

In order to explain why Diane opened her own firm, AD Solicitors, we need to go back just a step. As I have mentioned, Hurst & Co played a large part in her move and were the catalyst for her to take the next step.

We start in the spring of 1997. Diane and I are on our way to Portsmouth harbour for some R&R. We decided to take a weekend away to Bilbao. We started drinking from the time our backsides hit the train at Waterloo and it was a good job Portsmouth Harbour was the last stop otherwise we would have been on our way back to London before we realised we had to get off.

As we got into Portsmouth, the harbour was full of passengers with what looked like their empty suitcases. The significance of the empty cases would be clear later. Diane was tired and I was even more tired. We booked a cabin on the crossing so we could relax in peace and away from the partying of the other passengers. I didn't want to sleep on a bench or wash in the public convenience!

When we saw the size of the cabin, all we could do was look at each other and laugh. It was so small and the beds so close that if we turned over in the night, we would bang our heads together. We spent much of the cruise contemplating our fate and looking out to sea. Diane was becoming unsettled in her professional career even though she was now a partner at Hurst & Co and this trip was just before she announced to me she would be leaving. She wanted more.

I had just started a new job at RJW and was working as a PA to the managing partner. The job was OK, it paid well but it wasn't what I had trained to do all those years ago. I do regret having my family so early but I don't regret having my family. I felt as if I had missed out on the career I anticipated while at polytechnic and my parents had been so supportive and proud with what I had achieved. It was as if I was still experiencing a loss of expectation and I hadn't quite come to terms with that loss even after all these years. Francis never understood this as he thought it was normal for a woman to want to look after her family as his mother had done and her mother before her, but as she was the fourth wife of a very wealthy Nigerian businessman who could afford to keep four households, she didn't have to work and neither did she have any ambitions to do so.

I can understand how many ambitious young women who have children in their 30s after they have started to build their careers can feel that they have had to make a choice. Diane and I had discussed this ad nauseam. She believed then, and still does today, that the insurance market should have created a policy for young men and women that they could apply for once they had qualified – lawyers, doctors and the like – on which they could claim once they had children, either to use a lump sum to enable them to stay at home or to pay for childcare. Too much talent was being lost otherwise as good women and men were forced to stay at home and not return to work. The Women Lawyers Division at the Law Society runs a returners course dealing with the very issue of women wanting to return to work after a career break.

As I was always a fast typist (because I can't write), and because I understood the legal terminology to be used, a legal secretary/PA was perhaps the second best option for me. I didn't want to be a paralegal as that career choice would still have involved me staying in the office quite late at night and possibly working when I got home. My legal skills had been learnt many years ago and were now a little stale. Also the paralegals I knew were mainly female and from ethnic groups. The most annoying thing is that they were working in City firms earning reasonable money and working alongside colleagues who were on the way to becoming solicitors and doing the exact same work but they were not offered training contracts.

Trainees were on a pathway to qualification and paralegals were on a pathway to nowhere. What was that about? I really objected to the use of paralegals in this way as all it did was to keep a group of law graduates from qualifying into solicitors. The reasonable salaries they earned also meant they were tied if they wanted to leave as they would have to take a drop in salary to qualify in smaller firms. The policy in some firms at the time was not to offer training contracts to paralegals. A good PA in the City would earn a lot more money. I was earning more than Francis but I needed a break.

It was Sunday and the morning of the second day of the cruise. We would be arriving in Bilbao later that day. Diane and I decided we would go and have something to eat and then go to the cinema as there were several screens on board the ship. As we went in search of a restaurant, we noticed that all the bars were full and all the duty free shops empty of goods. There was very little booze and cigarettes left to buy. There was still a good amount of stock if you wanted perfume and chocolate!

We decided to eat quickly and then head to the duty free section to purchase our own supplies before it all ran out. When I think of this trip, I remind myself that you can now buy alcohol so cheaply in the supermarkets in the UK that there is now no need for booze cruises. I wonder what happened to P&O and all those companies and whether they had to cut their fleets as customers no longer took the short trips abroad to purchase their provisions.

We made our purchases and then went in search of a cinema. We had absolutely no idea what the film was about as we had purchased Coca Cola bottles from the vending machine, removed a third of the contents and filled them up with our duty free vodka. By the time the film started we had fallen asleep. We were no longer the party animals we used to be. We were too tired. I was used to a house of noise and the quietness made me relaxed and sleepy. There were no children asking me what was for dinner and there was no Francis asking where his glasses were, which were usually on top of his head! Bliss!

We arrived in Bilbao without incident and went on a tour of the area and were then left to our own devices. As it was nearing Easter, there was a procession through the streets. Diane and I looked at each other in horror when we saw a large group walking towards us with pointed blue hats covering their faces and white cloaks. These costumes were part of the reformation procession for Easter. The other passengers from the trip were very apologetic to Diane as the suits were vaguely Klan-like in appearance. Diane thought it was funny that these passengers were more embarrassed than her and very apologetic. The world had become so politically correct. To me all it meant was that the Klan was not original in their appearance.

Diane confessed while on the trip that she had wanted to do something new for quite some time and she referred to her mood as her 'creative patience' mood. She felt that if she left Hurst & Co she could unlock opportunities for herself elsewhere and before she knew it she was considering handing in her notice.

She had already met with a group of young Black lawyers who had the idea of opening a Black-owned commercial law firm in the City. Many thought that it was a good idea but when the crunch time came very few were prepared to give up their lucrative salaries in the City and start again. Diane and one other were prepared to do so.

Diane explained to me her thought processes which had helped her to make the decision to leave. She promised herself that if the business failed she would be prepared to rent her flat and move back in with her parents in order to save funds and make the business work. She also agreed that she would not take a salary for six months and further that she would raise £25,000.00 to open the practice. All of this was achieved. Diane wanted to follow her dream but at the same time felt conflicted with Hurst & Co who had been good to her, both professionally and privately, and she didn't really want to leave. She was torn.

A decision had to be made quickly on whether she was going to jump ship. We discussed this through the night while the boat was trying to rock us to sleep. Eventually we succumbed and must have fallen asleep at close to 5am. Diane woke up at about 6.30am to go to the bathroom and asked me if I wanted a drink. I said yes thinking she was going to go and get a coffee. She gave me a Bacardi and coke! At first I thought it was a joke but she was as sober as a judge! Rather than give it back to her, I just drank it and by breakfast we were both drunk again! We had, however, agreed on one thing: Diane would hand in her notice and take a leap of faith in herself and set up on her own. That is how easy the decision was made to move on.

Diane promised that once the firm was established she would invite me to join her as we had been childhood friends and we were sure that we could work together. I knew her better than anyone else. We both knew each other's personalities inside out. Diane was quite clear that she wanted to employ someone that she would be in a position to sack. She did not approve of employing family and friends because of who they were but because of what they could offer. We were both honest and frank with each other, and provided the recruitment process was carried out on an arm's length basis, with proper contracts, Diane would be happy to employ me. She didn't want her staff to challenge her decision in employing someone she knew so well.

I went to the opening party with Francis with high expectations and hopes that AD Solicitors would do well as I saw the firm as my future too. It was my way of getting back into the legal profession as I knew I would be given carte blanche to create a PA/paralegal position that I would not have been able to in other firms. Diane would trust me enough to give me some fee-earning work as well. As I was known to Diane as a good friend, I would also have the flexibility of looking after my ever increasing family. By 1998 I had three children.

The offices of AD were in a basement in Chancery Lane. When Diane gave out her business card, friends would look at her and ask, "Are you taking the piss? Chancery Lane?" The offices were not exactly the most salubrious in the area, but with a Chancery Lane address everyone in legal land knew exactly where it was and the prestige the address gave was second to none.

When I walked into the opening party I was met by a sea of lawyers who you could see were enjoying a drink, and the smell of fried chicken. There was clearly a party going on. A priest was in one room blessing the office and Diane was looking on in horror as he was using holy water to sprinkle around the room. She expected her computer to blow up at any time. Thankfully it didn't but we giggled from the incident... and possibly the rum!

Francis was uncomfortable. I am not sure why he didn't enjoy himself that evening but I realised later on the way home that he had felt uncomfortable as he believed that I could have done what Diane did but for him. He also felt if his cards were stacked differently he could have done it also. He lamented he had a better class degree than either Diane or me. This was a milestone confession for him. He somehow felt responsible for preventing my career from progressing in the way that we had all hoped when we were young and naïve in Wolverhampton. He found it difficult to express but felt he had somehow been the main player in taking my career from me and given me a family to look after instead. Outwardly he said nothing but I knew he was proud of Diane and also a little confused as his own career had not progressed as easily as hers. He resigned himself to the fact he knew he had what Diane did not. He had a family of his own and she did not.

Nevertheless, he vowed that he would use his family, friends and connections to help Diane in the new practice and I believed him. He seemed to be rejuvenated with the thought that at least one of the three musketeers, as we were often referred to in Wolverhampton, had managed to open their own firm.

As I now think of this party, it is apt that there was a priest as Diane and I were always very religious and spiritual and this had guided many decisions we have both had to make during our lives and would help Diane in particular in later life too.

It was a good omen that when AD opened on 5th January 1998 there was post waiting for Diane before she moved in. Everything in the firm was set up on a shoestring budget. The telephone and IT systems were put in by Diane's brother, and she could have not picked a cheaper spot in Chancery Lane unless she went into the bowels with the generator!

Within three years, AD had outgrown its Chancery Lane offices. It also coincided with a major redevelopment of the area and all leases in the building were coming to an end. The practice moved to Fetter Lane and rather than continuing as basement rats, the practice was now a penthouse queen. The views over London were stunning.

In 2003, the legal profession was moving in a different direction from when Diane and Francis qualified. There were a lot more firms becoming Limited Liability Partnerships (LLP) and this was something that Diane had decided AD should consider. In 2004 AD became an LLP. It was apparent at that time that the profession had slowly become a business. AD needed to become more business orientated in the way in which it ran its professional services.

A business is a legally recognised organisation designed to provide goods and/or services to consumers and generally earn a profit that will increase the wealth of its owners/partners/directors and grow the business itself. The law firm as a business entity has for years been formed by one or more lawyers to engage in the practice of law. It is only recently with the emergence of Alternative Business Structures (ABS) that non-lawyers were joining forces with practising lawyers to open businesses. The primary service of a law firm, however, is not necessarily to make a profit but to provide a legal service and to advise clients, who may be individuals and/or corporations, in relation to their legal rights and responsibilities. Law firms represent those individuals in both civil and criminal cases, business transactions and various transactions where legal advice and assistance is required. I could see that the definition of a business and definition of a law firm in 2004 were on a pathway to potential disaster.

Diane and I still saw the legal profession through rose-tinted glasses, as a profession and a vocation. The main purpose of the training at the College of Law was to help us supply the service, which was wholly apart from the expectation of the business. How then was Diane going to merge the two at AD?

It was quite fortuitous therefore that Diane was asked to attend a conference in Nigeria that year as part of the Commonwealth Lawyers Association (CLA) and asked to speak on this very topic – *The Business of Law*. She was rapidly beginning to understand that it was an ever changing game. I was still at RJW & Co and Diane asked me to help with research and typing for the conference in Nigeria – I loved a bit of moonlighting and Diane couldn't and still can't type for toffee!

My research confirmed that professional organisations and partnerships of the past were small and informal, with the exception of the very large City firms. In some European countries, professional practice still meant self-practice of a partnership with a few others – sometimes relatives. This I learnt was still the norm in Italy for instance. Now, by 2004, contemporary professionalism in England and Wales was no small affair and in many instances we had witnessed the emergence of a global professional service firm, employing thousands of people, both practitioners and administrators.

Most global professional services firms were not on speaking terms with the smaller practices nor did they resemble each other anymore. It was no surprise that over the next 10 years Legal Aid was to be battered left, right and centre; high street firms were to disappear if they did not merge; and the sole practitioner's group was ever decreasing in size as firms ran to merge with each other in order to survive and to compete for lucrative contracts. Who would have thought that in fewer than 10 years Legal Aid practitioners would be going on strike?

The problem with the very large professional services firms of this world was that they embodied an entrepreneurial spirit as they were mammoth businesses so profit and not service was the main aim. The high street practices had to acquire this spirit as there was still very much a place for them but they had to change. The larger law firms were continuously developing new markets, competencies, products, services – not for the man in the street but for corporate clients. I had worked in firms of all sizes and witnessed these changes right before my eyes. It is no wonder that the profession became the butt of many jokes as lawyers were often mistakenly seen as the fat cats of the City rather than the hard-working dedicated lawyers at the Legal Aid/high street/general practice end of the spectrum who were trying very hard to look after their practices and clients that needed and expected good legal services too.

As a PA, I had often worked on a temporary basis before I obtained full-time employment. I sometimes worked for City firms at night, in their document management departments essentially; I typed the documents at night, so they were ready in the morning for when solicitors returned to the office. Some of the solicitors would still be working when I started and their attitude and demeanour would be very different from the lawyers in smaller firms. The main difference was in stress level. The City appeared to take more out of you. I could see the difference between the large city corporations and the smaller Legal Aid firms that I had also worked in. The division between the two was scary.

Diane and I believed that what had happened as a result of these changes within the profession meant we were witnessing a commercialised version of legal services raising its head and the real premium for clients. Diane quickly realised AD had to deliver technical legal solutions which addressed the business needs of both corporate and individual clients.

It was not an easy time for any business owner, let alone Diane. The rules of professional conduct meant that ethical values and behavioural standards were key and the focal point. This does not fit or sit with and is diametrically opposed to, and a nemesis perhaps, of the world of business and commerce.

Professionalism is a way of controlling an occupation such as being a solicitor but the world of business was the Wild West. By 2004 the boundaries between professionalism, managerialism and entrepreneurship were merging, I think. To survive, law firms had to become more businesslike and commercial and the new hybrid, the professional services firm which had started in the City, had shown its dirty head in medium, small, high street and sole practices up and down the length and breadth of England and Wales.

There was more business and commercial outside pressure on the law firms to become bigger, better, more competitive, capture new markets, adopt matrix structures, multidisciplinary teams; different types of firms emerged with LLPs and soon to be alternative business structures. The purpose was to achieve more and this was not a good omen for professional services. Corners were cut so you had a skeleton staff and the main aim was to make profit for the partners/shareholders. Oh dear!

I discussed the topic with the senior partner at RJW & Co in preparation for Diane's paper and he agreed that law firms were becoming very sophisticated businesses. He was not surprised that law firms became businesses because it was the case in the 19th century. It was in the intervening years that the nature of the firm had changed and moved away from being a business.

As he was a frustrated historian, he explained the change to me as follows. He explained that the Joint Stock Companies Act 1844 and the Limited Liability Act 1855 allowed law firms to spiral. I was interested honestly but the history lesson made me want to yawn. I continued to take notes as I was sure Diane would find it fascinating. He went on. With the growth of the railways, this fuelled the dynamo that was becoming the legal profession. With the emergence of the railways nearly two hundred years ago, this meant that what lawyers did ordinarily was now changing and also how lawyers saw themselves. The introduction of the railways meant that legal, financial, technical, political and social factors had to be considered almost akin to management consultancy. I was taking as many notes as possible but this history lesson seemed to go on ad nauseam.

Every single sleeper had to be negotiated across the width and breadth of England. The land was already owned by someone. Rights of way were to be drafted and agreed. Each bridge and every station had to be built, planned, contracted, and completed. Money needed to be raised for every stage of the construction. This was big business. Lawyers were there to make real fortunes. Lawyers were ideally placed to reap the benefits of the industrial revolution and the rise of capitalism. They had an ability to circumnavigate government departments, parliamentary committees, financial houses, and influence legislation, all of which in turn regulated economic activity. Let us not forget that former Prime Minister Tony Blair, Justice Secretary Jack Straw and Bill Clinton, former President of the United States, were all successful lawyers. The same energy was rising again in the 1990s/2000.

Now that the history lesson had finished I could get back to the speech; I realised that what he had said was that law had gone full circle. We hadn't changed, we just became more sophisticated.

I had all the information I needed to crack on with at least the beginning and outline of a speech. I was energised. I quite liked doing the research and based it on my practical experience and knowledge.

Also I forgot to mention that Diane asked me to leave RJW and move to AD as her PA. OMG! I only had to give two weeks' notice and so I did and left!

I had the unenviable position of handing in my notice at RJW where I had become quite comfortable but tired. Francis did not agree with the move one bit. He felt that the dynamics between Diane and me in the workplace would not work because we were too close. Funnily enough Diane and I thought that because of the closeness it would work. Strange how our brains worked! I handed in my notice and moved anyway despite Francis's protestations.

CHAPTER 7

The Business of Law

LAW REPORTS

LAW REVIEW

CIVIL LAW

LEGAL DICTIONARY

So to the speech. Diane and I have only been working together at AD for a few weeks. In that time I had handed in my notice at RJW, moved to AD and completed the presentation. AD was now an LLP in 2004 and had taken up premises in Holborn.

Diane had worked with the Association of Women Solicitors for many years, becoming the Regional Chair of its London Group in 2006 and Chair of the National Group later. While on the committee she met many influential and inspiring lawyers, one of whom was an aspiring Nigerian Counsel who had closed her firm in the UK and opened a new one in Nigeria. Diane was invited by this colleague to speak at the Commonwealth Lawyers Association Conference in Nigeria. She was to talk about the business of law and we set about the task of finalising the presentation which I began to research many weeks ago before I left RJW.

As I mentioned, Diane had taken steps to change her business from a partnership to an LLP which in her mind was more akin to the business of a limited company. She decided that when she presented at the conference she needed to be as focused on the points she wished to make as she would be speaking to the Commonwealth lawyers who, in many aspects, were way behind the profession in England and Wales.

She challenged the Commonwealth lawyers to ask themselves what they felt the future of the legal profession meant to them, their careers, their firms and their practices, which she advised them would follow England and become big businesses. Diane felt that there were four main areas which governed law firms and we tried to explore these avenues in the preparation for the lecture. We had many arguments based on our individual personal experiences: Diane's as a business owner, mine as a PA/secretary whose career was in the same industry as Diane's and really not worlds apart.

Firstly, Diane outlined how she felt there was an increase in the commoditisation of legal services. She believed the profession was becoming more triangular in that specific reserved work was at the top of the triangle. Below was the work of importance but not threatening to the survival of the firm which was quasi-reserved. Then, you had repetitive or commodity work which was not reserved at the bottom. In this area of work, there were other individuals, companies and organisations coming into the market, trying to take away a piece of the lawyers' shrinking pie. Will writers for example were competing with probate practitioners on price.

Conversely, the higher the work moved from repetitive commodity to strategic, the more willing clients were to pay more money. However, the more the work moved from strategic to commodity, the volume of cases increased and clients were not willing to pay as much. There may be trouble ahead…!

Diane had already made the decision on whether AD continued to practice the commodity type work it had been practising since inception and which had increased in volume or to go for the more quasi-reserved work which was paying more but where there would be fewer cases. 'Less is more' was becoming a reality she said. Residential conveyancing was already in decline across the profession and at AD it had ceased. There was an increase in specialised litigation and employment matters as well as planning litigation cases generally and AD was making its mark in this area. As the author of this story, I can attest to the change in work type as I had to type it.

Notwithstanding what was happening in her backyard, the second point Diane wanted to make was in relation to the link between outsourcing and/or offshoring of legal services. She felt the Commonwealth lawyers present at the conference could be well placed to reap the benefits.

Diane explained how large firms were outsourcing contract drafting, legal research, patent applications and prosecutions, and e-document reviews amongst other things. Some firms were offshoring to places like China, India and Mauritius and there were opportunities for the Commonwealth English-speaking countries. I should point out I had travelled to Nigeria with Diane, so I was sitting in the conference listening to her speak which is how I know exactly what she was saying. In order to compromise with Francis, I had to stay with his aunt in Lagos before moving on to Abuja with Diane.

While at the conference, when looking at the blank faces in the audience I realised too late that Diane was talking about matters which were 10 years in front of some of these Commonwealth lawyers' business models. They were still grappling with the idea of advertising that England had left behind years ago, and outsourcing and offshoring only meant something to those larger legal communities of the Commonwealth such as India, Australia, New Zealand and Canada. Many representatives of African and other Indian subcontinent countries thought Diane was speaking a different language and was possibly indeed from another planet. The presentation was therefore word of wisdom to some and just words to others.

What really threw these lawyers from the smaller nations, however, was the point that the survival for these firms was the trend of the smaller firms that had begun to merge locally and internationally. Diane believed that firms needed to merge because of the overriding need to reduce overheads and costs which would amount to an increase in profit – or so she felt. Remember we had researched how law was/is a business. Law firms were now big businesses and profit was king or queen to many. If firms merged, there were then fewer firms to manage and at that time the SRA (Solicitors Regulation Authority) in England did not appear to be overly concerned with these mergers.

There is of course leverage of purchasing power when there are fewer firms about, but what was also happening was that there were deeper quality relationships with clients across borders and it was not unusual for medium-sized firms to have a presence in all of the continents. The smaller sole practitioners and high street firms were forced to join forces nationally and adopt the multi-office practices as a result of these changes.

Diane's fourth point to the packed auditorium explained what she referred to as the geographical expansion within the profession which she felt had become a problem and was diametrically opposed to her last point, but the difference was in scale.

Not only had law firms increased in size and decreased in number because of the mergers, the larger firms had now become more impersonal. Clients may be looked after by the head of a department but the work she saw was being carried out by his or her minion. There was more competitive pricing and it was increasingly unlikely that partners or heads of departments actually carried out most of the everyday mundane work, if at all, but they were expected to know all details of each client's case. In order to assist the partners and keep costs down, and to ensure that those who worked well benefited, the term 'associate' was born and these were divided into senior and junior associates. You then had salaried partners before you had equity. The corporate structure was continuing to raise its head in relation to the practice of law. Partnership decisions were now made by committees globally as that was more akin to the running of limited companies than partnerships. There was now increased travel for clients and solicitors. Because of the growth in large corporations, there was now more cross-border litigation dealing with multi time zones in one transaction.

As she looked up, Diane still felt that she had lost the attention of the majority of the audience but there was a contingent from South Africa and India who seemed to take on board her comments with ever increasing vigour. Cross-border litigation work had increased cross-cultural requirements including the multilingual capabilities of staff. Many of the larger Commonwealth countries had joined forces with other firms on other continents and were adjusting to these differences.

As English firms were expanding into different continents, Africa was revisited. The Black ethnic minority solicitors of the early 1990s when Diane qualified, who were few and far between, were now jumped upon because their particular skills were required in this multilingual, multi time zone, cross-border litigation that was becoming the staple diet of larger City firms. African lawyers were asked to look after the 'Africa desk' but without any realisation or understanding from the firms whether these lawyers were born in Africa like Francis, just African speaking or indeed whether they had lived there. They may just have had African names. This did not mean they understood every country in Africa – they are all different from each other – so that they could manage the Africa desk. These lawyers were set up to fail and had been given a poisoned chalice. How could you look after the Africa desk which would include Ghana, Kenya, Nigeria, all with different tribes, cultures, languages etc.?

The commoditisation of legal services, outsourcing and offshoring, the merging of firms locally and internationally, and the geographical expansion Diane had presented meant there was a clash and she saw a willingness of employees to relocate – regionally, nationally and internationally.

To relocate would enhance their careers. This in turn led to a seismic shift towards flexible working or the request for such which hitherto was confined to female lawyers who were going on maternity leave. Flexible working now became the norm for young lawyers of both sexes and was regularly asked for. Although the majority of lawyers in the room did not understand Diane's vision as they had not lived it, they did recognise the potential and movement of legal services in England would be coming their way, and soon!

After the presentation had finished, Diane was in the ladies' room and was approached by a local Nigerian lawyer who asked her to chair a splinter group on the business stream that she had just finished speaking on. The speaker allocated had dropped out at short notice. Diane agreed.

Diane accepted the invitation to speak at the splinter group and took me along with her as she wanted me to take notes as she had a feeling there could be a business opportunity coming up and she wanted my view on it.

The South African and Indian lawyers who had attended her earlier presentation were heartened by her view that the world was opening up for lawyers internationally and these English-speaking countries of the Commonwealth could assist England and Wales. However, they questioned her on what she felt were the characteristics of a 21st century lawyer as a result of all this movement and where she felt the profession had become in her eyes more commercial and businesslike.

Diane was clear in her answer to the question. The 19th century view of stability, security, and long-term career paths had gone and was now replaced with the re-emergence of aggressive competitive opportunities and the self-initiated career paths. In her mind the 21st century lawyer must be:

a) Prepared to move repeatedly throughout his or her career which hitherto was frowned upon. She likened lawyers to Premier League footballers and were all 'for the fame, glory and money!'

b) The 21st century lawyer must effectively market and promote himself/herself in order to win business. She asked what was their USP (unique selling point). If you don't have one, what is your use to these firms and their need for profit? How will you sell them and yourself?

c) Lawyers were becoming less of team players as they strove to achieve the team of 'Me/I' (there is no I in the word team). The close-knit world of the firms I had started to work with as a PA many years ago appeared to be changing when people were becoming less collegiate.

The small audience before Diane and me recognised these changes and traits within themselves and their colleagues but they were struggling with the idea that at the same time they needed to be accessible, responsive, manage their clients' expectations without falling foul of their regulators, run a business, and make a profit. It was too much as some just wanted to practise law. They had to meet and exceed deadlines and give 100%, 100% of the time, and stay on the right side of the profession. As always, lawyers needed to provide correct, practical, useful advice but also be creative in an effort to assist client businesses. Notwithstanding this, the regulator expected firms to remain discreet (keep clients' confidentiality) and abide by the rules of professional conduct, at the same time producing the best results for profit-led owners. The new 21st century lawyer was a different business animal from the business lawyer who practised following the industrial revolution and the expansion of the railways. What had we created? They wanted an answer so they could prepare themselves for the shift.

Diane tried to explain that it was the individual's track record and that of the firm and their reputation above all else that was paramount: their accessibility, fee structure, firm strategy and the treatment of clients. There was no one quick fix.

Firms had to become introverted and segment their clients in order for the firms to understand their clients' needs better. She likened the trend to the use of clubcards issued by Tesco (which again confused the group as some had never heard of Tesco!). As the shopper purchased, their likes and dislikes were recorded on the clubcard. You were then sent brochures to increase your purchasing in those areas because you are given clubcard points. A computer tells you what your preferences are! Law firms were doing the same on a different level. They were setting up seminars for those clients with similar areas of interests or businesses that were of interest to the group, in order to get more business from the group.

Diane left the lawyers with more questions than answers but she concluded with the view that law as a business is not a new phenomenon. It has been around for quite some time but it is the role of the professional within the business which has changed as the profession has moved from professional services to the provision of legal services industry that it is today. Law firms were dismissing partners in an effort to be economical. The old professional quality of the 'contract of mutual responsibility with partnerships' was being replaced by the ugly looking sense of 'expendability of individual talent'. Diane felt this was counterproductive to the progression of the profession as we knew it but it was the way we were going.

Because of the reduction in staff, talent was lost as a result of the increased rounds of law firm redundancies. Diane asked the audience not to make the same error. Professional services firms are still only as good as the people who make them up which includes those who are trained through or who have transferred to those businesses. She pointed out that people like me were important and then explained I was her PA before anyone offered me a job as a lawyer!

Training and recruiting talent had to be the number one priority in these difficult times but that was not what Diane was witnessing. The need for profit was driving firms in the opposite direction. Firms missed the point that to motivate individuals and retain their services for the businesses gain, the only sensible answer would be to pay staff more and incentivise them so that the future generation of lawyers is what they (the profession) wanted it to be.

The new 21st century lawyer was willing to move and they would move for the money. Future generations of lawyers would not be doing commoditised work and will grow up concerned with money rather than partnership and service. The Commonwealth communities could reap this benefit. The larger law firms would start to move the way of investment banks. The movement would inevitably change the hierarchy in a professional services firm and the role of the partner. This could very well be the end of the team players as Diane knew it. This movement had already started in the larger Commonwealth countries and Diane urged the smaller African and Caribbean countries to take heed and not follow the same mistake. Who knew what the changes Diane had foreseen would mean: clashes between solicitors and the regulator in the UK?

You can't be a businessperson and a lawyer comfortably. Business requires you take calculated risks. As regulated professionals, we can't.

The group were appreciative of Diane's honesty. They wanted Diane to write business plans for them and consultancies going forward. As Diane thought, there would be a business opportunity and there it was. She had now secured some work in assisting these Commonwealth lawyers and getting paid to do it. The key was that she wanted to help them and would have done it for free but as they wanted to pay… The bigger they were, she felt the more they would want to reach out, instruct her or even refer clients to the UK. It was a win-win situation for AD. Sometimes you have to think out of the box on how you can help others help you!

Diane was beginning to enjoy the talks and presentations for the CLA as she increasingly felt that was more her calling than the actual carrying out of the legal work. She felt her experience was of more benefit to the profession in an advisory role. It was coincidental that the following year she was invited to speak at a conference in Jamaica and asked to speak on the topic of *Technology and the Law: Tool or Master.*

Crikey, I was beginning to feel jealous of her celebrity but I knew, no matter what, I was going to Jamaica too! Technology was a topic I could get my teeth into. I agreed with Diane that I would prepare the first draft of her presentation and she could legalise it or 'sex it up' for the lawyers for the conference. Finally I got to use my brain and experience to prepare the first full draft!

Here goes!

CHAPTER 8

Technology and the Law: Tool or Master

LAW REPORTS

LAW REVIEW

CIVIL LAW

LEGAL DICTIONARY

I am really looking forward to preparing the technology presentation for Diane as it is my bag. I have been trained for this as a PA and probably have more experience than lawyers in this area. It is strange over the years that I have never been asked my opinion on this area by fee-earners. All they think is that I just type and do not realise that I can also comment and have a brain just like them. God, lawyers can be annoying!

Lord, it's another Monday and Diane is leaving in a month for the Caribbean where she is presenting her paper on *Technology and the Law: Tool or Master*. We had a week to complete the research and prepare the paper as the Jamaican organisers wanted the presentation to be proofread by them and sent three weeks before the conference.

I worked closely with the IT team to help introduce systems to RJW & Co and then latterly into AD. We use IT every day. Between the two of us, Diane and myself, we must be able to cobble together something that is reflective of the importance – or not – of technology.

Diane provides me with her outline as to what she would like to have in the presentation. I recall that she revamped the IT system quite extensively at AD because she wanted to work from home as she was going through the process of adopting. Yep, you heard me, adopting. If you want something done, ask a busy person!

For her 40th birthday, Diane decided she would buy herself several gifts so she bought a convertible car and a Mont Blanc pen that she had always wanted amongst other things. She had also decided to take the plunge of going through the process of adopting a child.

It was widely reported that Afro-Caribbean professionals did not put themselves forward for bone marrow transplants, blood donation, adoption or fostering. So Diane would be a gift to them, right? Nope!

Diane contacted a private organisation rather than the local authority, one that specialised in finding placements for children from an ethnic minority background. After years of pursuing our own individual paths, me with four children, I wanted Diane's life but she also wanted mine. The grass always seems greener on the other side, right?

Diane completed the adoption process. The course was rigorous when you consider you could have a child yourself quite easily and without numerous checks returned to work almost immediately. I did… where Francis allowed. Diane took the experience in a positive way and felt that it would be a fight for the survival of the fittest. Those applicants who really wanted a child had to get to the end of the process before they could be successful, but they had to jump through the many social services hoops first.

The adoption process was not made for someone like Diane who constantly questioned why, like a five-year-old, to every question she was asked. This then led to her motives being questioned. Notwithstanding the many hoops, Diane passed the adoption panel and was unanimously approved as an adopter but the problem came with the matching panel. The children's social workers wanted someone who was prepared to stay at home for six months. They did not recognise that Diane ran a business or if they did, they did not care. They did not look positively on solicitors, I understand, and felt them to be relentless slaves to the hourly rate.

If Diane had given birth to her own child, she would probably be back at her desk within six weeks. She asked social services for assistance and whether they could recommend any organisations within their catchment area in south London that would be able to assist, at least, so that she could go back to work two days a week. They said no. She had to stop working for six months as they could not put a child from the system back into an institution when they may have already come from one.

Diane produced a list of her monthly income and expenses and asked social services to confirm if they would be in a position to pay for her expenses if she were to take six months off. This may have happened if she found a child but she had to agree six months so it was a vicious circle; they were not in a position to assist her financially at that stage and before a child was found. There was an impasse.

On the one hand social services wanted Black ethnic minority professionals to engage in the adoption process but on the other hand they were putting obstacles in their way, and certainly in Diane's way, to allow her to achieve the goal as a single adopter. I supported Diane during this period and know she was made to feel inadequate and a leper for wanting to work. To be Diane and the best mother she could be, she needed to work. She promised she would never do the adoption course again, and whilst the social workers were trying to fit square pegs into square holes only, it appeared they could not think out of the box.

Diane's son was in care somewhere whilst social services appeared to pussy-foot about a six-month timeframe and in circumstances where they were not in a position or able or indeed willing to assist.

Diane found the whole episode challenging and a personal failure. She had opted for Black boys. Black boys tend to stay in the adoption system a lot longer than any other group and certainly when compared to Black girls. It was therefore strange that these obstacles were being placed before her without any resolution or discussion on how this process could be managed to help Diane help herself and a child. We both felt that little progress could be made. I felt enormous sympathy for Diane as she would have been an excellent parent, and although she did not have a child of her own, I had watched her look after her younger sister Nora-Jean and her other sister's children and although she could be harsh, it was clear she would protect them. Isn't that what a parent's primary role is – to love and protect their children no matter what?

It was against this background of change in her personal life that Diane had invested a lot of time and effort in technology at AD because she felt it would be beneficial to work from home remotely if she was successful with the adoption process. She even changed her business model for the child and extended her home to get the place ready. She renovated the roof space. But that still wasn't enough. Social services wanted her to give up 'Diane the working woman'.

Not yet put off, Diane had progressed the development of the remote access system so that the partners were able to dial in remotely from home to work. The dictation system moved from physical tapes to a digital format, and the firm interviewed for a practice manager whose primary role was to take over a large amount of the administrative duties that Diane had assumed since inception of the practice.

The position of practice manager was never satisfactorily resolved as the other partners wanted to combine the position with a financial controller and the person who accepted the position could not be conversant in both. Although he professed to be fully capable of handling the administration, it was soon clear he was really only interested in finance. To make matters worse, the adoption process fizzled out and Diane was left believing that AD had taken her life but had also taken her future as she resigned herself to not having her adoptive son and remaining forever linked to the business.

Taking these implementations at AD on board, I thought about what had been introduced into the AD environment within the last few years that could assist with the upcoming Commonwealth Lawyers Association Conference and, in particular, Diane's lecture on technology and how it had impacted within the legal profession or on the legal professional.

The question really is: is technology a 'tool' that can assist with the tasks and operations that legal practice entails or is it a 'master' in that the profession depends entirely on its use and development and cannot survive at all without the use of the resource?

I am acutely aware of the administrative needs of a firm as I was a pivotal member of that group. The legal profession, in an effort to become a business, now had a lower proportion of legally trained workers or knowledge workers as a total of all staff. This is true when you compare lawyers to other professions. As a consequence, there was a huge reliance on the recruitment of staff for admin and support services.

Generally, it was believed that lawyers did not make adequate use of the available technology and administrative support for their businesses and the delivery of legal services to their clients. It was only when other organisations were moving into the legal arena, e.g. will writers, employment services, licensed conveyancers etc., that lawyers became more open minded and proactive. Lawyers are usually reactive as a group and complain after things had already happened or started to happen to them. Lawyers continuously looked at their belly buttons to remove the fluff whilst other groups had moved into the arena and taken a part of the available work. Lawyers had to re-emerge as a better business and technology was looked upon as the possible assistance in this regard – a quick fix, I think.

The introduction and expansion of technology within legal practices was seen as a way to improve convenience and efficiency in line with the trend of bigger, better, stronger. In the process, it appeared technology and law became a *dependency* relationship rather than a *tendency* relationship and the increased use of technology was an absolute necessity for the continued existence of the profession, or so I thought as a PA. I really felt that to understand technology one needed to understand the changes in the way in which lawyers went about their business from the 20th to the 21st century and what a leap that was. I had already examined the business of law when assisting Diane on a previous presentation and so the two topics are inextricably linked. I therefore felt comparing the 20th and 21st century lawyer would be helpful from a historical analysis.

The life of a 20th century lawyer I learnt could be summarised in five main areas:

1) Firstly, the life of a lawyer had not always been the way it is today. They don't have to have face-to-face meetings today. Previously, before the onset of modern technology, lawyers had to do a lot more labouring and cases would take much longer to be resolved for a client. A typical day may begin with a lawyer coming into the office to be greeted in person by a new client. There were no emails, telephones, fax, Skype, internet as a means of making contact, it was all done in person.

2) Secondly, once the enquiry was made, the lawyer would research that area of law by finding the leading precedents of the day. This may have involved a trip to the Law Library to find the relevant case law and books as then there were no resources online or databases allowing for the quick and easy access of case law as there are now. In the 21st century a PA, or even a lawyer if that way inclined, could find a case within seconds.

3) Thirdly, any research required would have to be done manually and by trawling through books. This meant making notes relevant to a particular

case in hand. Once the typewriter was introduced, this improved standards of presentation and reduced misunderstandings when documents were transferred to others in manuscript. Just think for a second, there was no word processor! Any correspondence between a lawyer and clients or third parties was in writing or in person. As a result, there were regular trips to the client's home, place of work and in some criminal cases, to prison. With the introduction of the telex machine quickly followed by the mobile telephone, fax and now email and SMS, this process has sped up. These other forms of communication have drastically reduced the amount of travelling time for the lawyer, just merely to communicate with the outside world. I am not sure which I would prefer if I was practising. I know for sure Diane would like to go back to the 20th century and hide just to get some work done and cut off 21st century means of communication... if only for an hour.

4) Fourthly, the most arduous task of the 20th century lawyer was to trawl through the archived files to find that elusive document. One document to find, often the one amongst thousands. Good organisation and management of paper files and maintaining the integrity of those files was therefore paramount to the efficient business of a lawyer. This is made much easier today with the introduction of electronic archives which I manage on a day-to-day basis and teach others to manage too.

5) The fifth major challenge in the 20th century was to produce reliable and irrefutable evidence. The gathering and adducing of evidence was probably the biggest of all challenges to the profession as there was little scientifically tested or computer-generated evidence which could have been corroborated by experts – for instance forensics in criminal cases. DNA does not stand for Do Not Answer! It is a relatively recent phenomenon.

I pondered at my own position as a PA and the way in which I assisted partners and fee earners of the firm and was surprised at the list!

With the introduction of PCs came the internet, word processing, Excel, Publisher etc. I am able to print documents and letters easily, and even if I make one error, the amendment and resultant printing can take but a few seconds. I can print in colour or black and white. I can scan documents for storage and management. I have a fax machine which quickly followed the telex which I vaguely remember. Telephone systems have improved beyond belief. There are now voiceover IP systems. There is mobile technology as well as Blackberrys. The accounts departments are assisted with accounting and billing software to enable monthly reconciliations to be a simple task as it is a regulatory requirement. We had the introduction of expert software in specialist areas, to manage particular files and procedures. With the introduction of webinars for interactive training software, this helped multinational firms save on costs and also the lawyer's time. Lawyers did not have to leave their office.

My own work is now more digital, and with the introduction of digital dictation the work produced by the fee earner is clearer and more concise and can be sent over time zones and continents. It was convenient for work to be sent back a time zone and for it to be worked on overnight while London slept.

With the introduction of digital dictation, my typing speed increased, I can then photocopy what needs to be done once printed and I can photocopy in combination with fax, printer and scanner in one machine. If I don't like what I've printed, and for confidentiality reasons, I can shred it and not have to set it alight to ensure the contents are destroyed. As I make this short task list, I stop and think what happened to confidential papers before the introduction of the shredder and how was client confidentiality achieved? Confidentiality is paramount today and the Solicitors Regulation Authority would not be happy if this was breached. Wow, this list took me several minutes to make and you can see just how it has helped me going forward.

I am energised by the preparation of my list and I now start to type.

The most common uses of technology for the vast majority of law firms regardless of size really can be confined to a few core uses in addition to the list I prepared above:

a) Time recording. I hate it, so does every other lawyer I have met. Time recording can creep over to their private lives as I have witnessed. They leave themselves enough time to read bedtime stories to their children in units of six minutes each. They leave themselves time to speak with their families in units of six minutes each. Diane has often referred to the time recording as 'lie sheets' as you can list the time spent on a transaction and because each unit is calculated in units of six minutes each, it is the most efficient method for firms to profit but not necessarily for the client! Even if two minutes of time is spent on a matter, the client is charged six.

b) Accountancy systems have helped solicitors to put in checks and balances to ensure that accounting rules and systems are adopted and followed by all as required by the Solicitors Regulation Authority.

c) Word processing has helped streamline and introduced more efficient methods within my daily work. Bearing in mind that I may now be able to produce a document faster, what do I do with the rest of my time? I have no idea.

d) As AD occupies an office in Central London, space is a premium. Archiving has saved a lot on valuable space and provided a far more efficient and better organised storage of files and documents. Some firms operate virtual archives and everything is scanned and stored. Paper files are becoming a thing of the past whereas previously papers and books were part of the lawyer's DNA.

For all the positives of technology, there is one major drawback in that the system can fail. If it fails and you haven't backed up the system, you are stuffed. It is imperative to maintain and update a backup system including a backup power supply to operate the equipment in the event of a loss of power. A failure to plan may see the 21st century lawyer plunge back into the 20th century having to do research and communicate in ways that are completely alien to them. You may plan to fail. I laugh as I make this point as I am absolutely certain Diane would have heart failure if this was the case and she woke up 100 years ago.

I had the outline for the presentation! As Diane is a business owner and giving a talk to business owners, we had to focus on the way in which technology could bring in business for AD, to improve service for the clients and the management of staff and the business generally. I examined each in detail and my research revealed the following.

If you looked at the way in which technology brought in business for you, we now have a client database and analysis which is a collection of all clients represented with an analysis of their needs and requirements recorded on a PC. We work smarter to retain clients but don't have to work harder. In order to market clients, we have access to their websites or business cards which are produced in a Word version. We check conflicts with various clients very easily by searching our databases. Previously we would have had to trawl through reams of paper.

AD had outsourced its reception duties to a call centre. It had external call stations contracted to take enquiries and transfer the calls to fee earners. AD made valuable use of the call centre which was located miles from where the physical premises of AD was situated in Central London. This reduced staff costs and overheads. It meant that the workload of the solicitors within the office and of the PA reduced as we did not have to take numerous enquiries. Enquiries were taken by the call centre and relayed to the relevant fee earner, thereby saving time. It was clear that partners wanted a bum on a seat to pay for the business, rather than the business pay for a bum on a seat which was the case if someone was sitting in the office answering a telephone all day and not earning any money when someone could be sitting in that seat and doing billable work. What is the value of the receptionist in the office? Very little, I think.

The most important area in which technology had assisted the business of law was in client care. Technology had helped in document drafting and assembly. In my position as a PA, I was able to use word processing, Excel software and due diligence could be completed abroad at a much lower cost than in England. We can now research for clients online with our online databases or subscription journals and periodicals. There is a huge number of government archive websites available with online experts, and case law and databases which lawyers can use. Law firms utilise technology to help with the indexes of client matters so I am able to store letters and documents chronologically. The e-filing of documents through government and court websites is second to none. I can issue a draft claim within half an hour whereas it would have taken quite a lot of research and possibly not been done by me as a PA, but by a solicitor just 10 years ago. There are thousands of court documents which can be purchased online or obtained for free. These systems are available 24/7. With the introduction of the central processing registry in Northampton, you can even officially serve by this method so if we prepare documents electronically, they will be processed and served by the court faster.

From an operational perspective, I considered that technology would assist with the commoditised work and services even though it was not an area that AD had pursued. These proprietary systems were useful for human resources, banking and regulatory compliance. I was uncomfortable with this as I felt some firms no longer employed paralegals/PAs based in the UK because of these commoditised tasks which could be outsourced cheaply abroad. Diane thought this made good business sense, but as my job was on the line I did not. You don't have to go to an English-speaking country to get things done if you do not wish to as some people will use machine translations of certain information from official documents and there are some full-scale bilingual websites. Notwithstanding this, there is still huge scope for forward-thinking law firms to employ technology to profit from language issues which may arise with their clients.

How did I ever find that one document out of 20,000? I can now search for a selection of words and come up with the answer in minutes. Once found, the electronic distribution of information is quick and easy through emails, memos, fax, e-flyers and business cards, and clients themselves are becoming more sophisticated as they grow up with technology and become aware of the benefits of case notes, virtual deal rooms or virtual boardrooms to bring in suppliers and extranet facilities within their practice.

There are automated case management systems accessible online and permitted representatives and their clients to check the progress of their case and update their case. We don't even have to get up and see clients now as we have video conferencing and Skype, so technically bills should be reduced, right? Nope, someone must pay for the investment!

Computer-generated demonstrative evidence has grown. I came across a Canadian case which was the first civil case in Ontario where a computer-generated image was introduced. By the time an expert was retained, the Defendant Road Authority had removed a mound of earth that had otherwise obscured visibility at the intersection and where the accident occurred. Using a couple of still photographs taken by an adjustor before the earth was removed, a company was able to reinsert the obstruction, not into a still photograph but into a video showing what the driver would have seen as he approached the intersection. Technology was important in relation to electronic discovery. How can this not be a tool?

If we look at a simple memo in paper form, all you would see is the paper in front of you. The electronic version, however, in Word format, would show all the useful information contained in the memo which would have been missed – for instance, the date it was actually prepared and not the date the creator said it was prepared! Even the Courts are now conducting case management conferences online with judges and all parties sitting in their own offices. Crikey, we are chained to our desks! As I am conducting this research I am beginning to feel that technology is a great tool but it does appear to have taken over legal practice completely and quite masterfully; we could never turn the clock back. Diane did not feel the paper would be rounded unless we looked at technology in relation to the management of staff. Although I could speak about this, Diane was better placed to do so.

Diane examined financial management and the way in which accounting and billing software had assisted finance teams with online expenditure, tracking the cost of a case and by requesting service providers to submit invoices through a proprietary billing system. Firms quickly realised that a competitive advantage was obtained if the firm could ensure its invoices could be issued through a client specified means. Firms would benefit from guaranteed payments within set time frames and eliminate the need to apply credit control resources in the service to that particular client. Staff were able to keep in contact with each other through emails, external internet, memos, the internal intranet, electronic diaries and schedules which meant that no one could hide from Big Brother who was certainly watching you!

Outlook has the ability to access multiple diaries to arrange appointments over a group of people. Previously, I would ring everyone, make a list of their available dates then work out which days were available then go back to everyone to confirm, by which time diaries would have filled up. Now, all I need do is send out an invitation through Outlook and the available date is agreed without me doing anything further. Easy peesy lemon squeezy! In the old days, this could have taken me a day to organise.

Storage, archiving, filing and deed management is probably the biggest area of assistance for me in my daily work where files and deeds are drafted using word processors and spreadsheets. Both may be archived electronically on the hard drive. I can protect work confidentiality as computers are gateways through which we communicate with the public, by using PC usernames and log in accounts for each staff member, thereby creating security and accountability for errors and breaches. Even at AD these steps were key to protecting the firm and clients.

Digital dictation could be outsourced and in fact at that time AD used Night Office and latterly AAT Network who were based in England, but for any work sent after 7 o'clock at night, Night Office automatically sent the dictation to New Zealand where people were already up. With my assistance, AD had already introduced remote working as a result of Diane's initiatives surrounding the greater need for remote working when considering adopting. We were considering using the Citrix system which we knew larger firms were using to log into their offices anywhere in the world. This package proved far too expensive for a firm of AD's size to implement. On reviewing the software for the presentation, I realised it was a fantastic system to be implemented where users were able to view all applications in a safe environment as if they were sitting in front of their desk – but not for AD as it was too costly.

Webinars were introduced. Remote seminars were prepared for employees of multinational companies and produced via the internet. This was cheaper than sending staff away and only a few hours were lost rather than a whole day. Members of staff could bill more as everything would turn to profit as they were kept in the office! The Luddite culture that once lurked within the legal profession had declined and it is almost a mandatory requirement that newly qualified solicitors are IT literate. I surmise as I am drafting this paper that the use of a specialist PA like me may be eliminated within the next five to 10 years in many firms. PAs would go into remote working. Solicitors would be trained to operate and manage electronic mediums, with technology being an integral part of the law. Perhaps I may need to carve out a new position for myself! But as what? Even PAs as I knew them were reducing in number and our jobs were changing as everything was becoming remote.

In order to produce a balanced paper I needed to find negative influences of technology. I did feel that the Commonwealth as a rapidly developing region could influence and affect all areas of business including the legal sector because of the time difference and the fact that English was their first language. They should have, as the Indian subcontinent had, identified various prospects and opportunities offered by technology for improving and advancing legal practice as well as acknowledging current uses. There was, however, resistance due to the lack of awareness and unfortunate experience where things have gone wrong. This made solicitors sceptical but their scepticism was unfounded. You do need good IT backup in this regard and with the implementation of PC Anywhere, your IT support does not have to be sitting in your office twiddling his/her thumbs before something goes wrong. This is great for smaller firms with limited cash flow as IT specialists could be shared.

I had noticed an unwillingness of partners to invest as it affects the bottom line. Why don't they invest to make life easy for staff that should be there to make a profit for them? This is short-sighted. A fairly simple package for accounts and file management combined could cost upwards of £10,000.00 and is out of the bracket for most small firms. Diane and I agreed that there was a pressure for change on lawyers. The pressure came from clients, competitors and recruits.

I recalled Diane's reference to the 21st century lawyer whom she likened to a Premier League footballer or indeed a Formula One driver with sponsorships (clients). The lawyer would go to any firm (club/team) that was going to pay him or her more money. If you were going to pay money and you had all the systems in place, then the practice of law is so much easier. However, even those firms that had introduced huge technological advances in many areas have often failed because they failed to implement the relevant introductions with the sufficient amount of training.

It is no use having the best system in place if your staff do not know how to use it. If all firms use completely different systems, then when a fee earner moves from one firm to another, there is a whole new set of systems to be learnt and the recruitment process is so much more difficult at this level as staff need to be updated continuously and the process is designed to fail. Maybe there should be standardised regulatory software companies that should get together with the Solicitors Regulation Authority and prepare legal practice packages for small, medium and large firms which firms must adopt, so it is easier for staff when they move and can understand these proprietary systems.

I sit and ponder but still feel the paper is too positive. I felt incumbent to end on some negative influences which flowed from the introduction of technology, so I listed just a few. It was worrying that the only negative I had was that it could all fail in the absence of a backup. My list wasn't very long.

Firstly, there are cases where technology doesn't work especially if it is used as a prop, for instance in court where its failure is designed to embarrass. Enough said.

Secondly, the 21st century lawyer cannot now hide from clients, colleagues or the office. If a client cannot make contact with you via the switchboard they will call your mobile, landline, send you a text or an email. It is almost as if the lawyer must now be available 24/7. You can't hide in the library where there is no phone. This has added stress to the lives of the lawyers and meant early retirement for some.

Thirdly, and I can vouch for this as I had seen Diane's reaction when she received something with a stamp on it, she very rarely received letters. Everything is electronic. We recall one client asked what the best way to get hold of her was and she replied, "Send me something with a stamp on it because I don't receive them anymore and so read them first!"

Fourthly, as a result of the internet and increased correspondence by email in the last 10 years, this has sped up the process of the actual provision of legal services. I suspect there may have been a corresponding increase in claims due to the sheer pressure of answering emails too quickly. I asked Diane to check with the Solicitors Regulation Authority and they were not able to confirm whether they had any records on this point at that time as the question was too specific. Cyber space etiquette meant that emails should be answered in a certain number of hours whereas you could rely on a letter being answered in a number of days. If you don't answer emails promptly, there is a perceived lack of communication and therefore service, or so the client believed, which could lead to a claim for inadequate professional services.

I had noticed as a PA that clients would contact a solicitor by phone to say they had sent an email because although they knew it was instantaneous, they weren't sure if it was delivered. This put pressure on both the client and the solicitor. A client may feel that his/her solicitors may not be providing a good service because the solicitor was not answering emails by return. If we don't have our 'out of office' on, the client is expecting a response immediately. The converse is that once an email is received there is an urgency for the solicitor to reply before they have thoroughly reviewed the point, I noticed. Diane adopted the stance that unless an email required an immediate response of fewer than two sentences, it should be answered the following day or indeed during the ordinary course of business.

Diane believed the number of work-related emails received on a daily basis far exceeded letters and at least 20 times more emails than the letters received 10 years ago. HR departments in larger law firms monitored staff emails and internet access. Many firms had to introduce an authorised user guide preventing solicitors' use of certain sites. Big Brother is watching you! Even I had drafted an authorised user guide for AD which in comparison was a small firm.

Due to all of this speed in access and communication, I recalled reading a book where everything in the last 200 years had been introduced to speed up time and I wanted to refer to it in the presentation but could not remember the name. The microwave was introduced to speed up the cooking process; the digi-box to ensure that we could look at films on demand, rather than wait for them to be shown in the next cycle at Christmas or Easter. Everything was moving too fast which in turn increased the stress of life and the stress of the workplace for the lawyer. I believed everyone should be trying to slow down and take more holidays and work efficiently but technology had meant that things had sped up to such an extent that the human body just couldn't cope with the speed. I was left with a real sick feeling that if I didn't control technology it would control me. I remember an incident when I had left my mobile phone at home and had to ask my mother to go to my home to bring the phone to the office. Why would I do this when my mobile phone replicated my Outlook box at work which was on the computer screen in front of me! My mobile could take messages and if I missed a call I could return it later. I then had to fix that problem as I believed it was a sickness.

In recent years, there has been an increase in Voiceover Internet Protocol (VOIP) phone systems which I am particularly pleased about as a lot of my time was previously spent on the phone taking messages. I love new technology. VOIP is all the rage at home and work and it is increasingly used because of the benefits of the system.

Firstly, the systems require no or little additional equipment as all you need is an internet connection. Secondly, you need no additional engineers to maintain the system and therefore there is no extra maintenance cost to the business as repairs and upgrades are carried out through the Cloud – a virtual system that adds updates quickly and swiftly without interruption to the business. From my point of view, and with looking after a group of PAs, it is great to be updated at the same time and we can then advise the partners, fee earners, trainees, paralegals and support staff of what updates have taken place and offer them training.

Fourthly, wherever you are online in the world, you have access to the system. You can redirect for free phone numbers, change message alerts, download, call data whilst on the toilet seat if that is what you desire! The beauty for me as a PA is I don't have to take the calls for the solicitors/fee earners in the office and this system can receive messages out of hours, thereby saving on PA time as well as the call centre time and costs that AD uses during the working day. Even for a firm of AD's size, VOIP is looked upon positively and call centres may be going out of business. The only thing that is slowing this process down is that clients actually want to speak to a living person.

Fifthly, for large corporations, this system works for employees spread over buildings and also companies and where there are multiple time zones. You know when the recipient is online and so you can call them through Skype immediately when they log on. My mother has cottoned on to this very annoyingly, so I leave my computer online all the time just to confuse everybody!

Lastly, this system is very flexible and with the auto-receptionist to greet callers, the role of the receptionist of days gone by, and certainly one of my tasks as a PA, has become redundant. This leaves the solicitor and PA the time to focus on their service to their clients and with the pay-as-you-go models operating today, it is very cost-effective and cheaper than the traditional telecoms systems with ADSL or ISDN 30 lines and with practically zero set-up costs. This has not resulted in costs saving to the client.

The scary part of my research was the realisation that the emergence of new technologies appeared to be having a disruptive effect on the established legal markets as we know them. Diane explained to me when we were going through the final draft that the City police and the fraud squad have a tough and steep learning curve to keep up with cybercrime and criminal activities as a result of the new technologies. Law enforcers, lawyers as well as the police and the CPS, had to create new procedures as technology was moving much faster perhaps than law enforcement and central government could respond to.

As a result, criminals were succeeding in opening up loopholes. Criminals including former practising solicitors, accountants and other professionals come up with new and varied ways of allowing technology to help them commit criminal acts as solicitors assist their clients. It is arguable that the current way of operating and detecting crime may mean it is time to rethink strategies and habits which have arisen as a result of some legal and social norms about what is possible!

Anyone under the age of 30 is generally computer literate. We all need the minds of these same whizz kids to assist law enforcement in an effort to combat technology and the rise in crime based on new technologies. White collar crime departments in City law firms were expanding... we must get that into the paper! Diane will expand on this point as I don't have the skill or knowledge but she had the contacts with her colleagues in the industry.

On doing her own research, Diane came across a London newspaper in September 2008 which confirmed that if you were pining for the internet then you were 'discomgoogleated'. We are not even sure if this is a word but it sounded good! Diane felt this must go into the paper somehow as the word appeared to confirm that the internet had pervaded our lives to such an extent that this new word attempted to describe our withdrawal symptoms when we couldn't get our daily internet hit.

Discomgoogleated was defined as a feeling of distress and anxiety suffered by people who cannot Google what they want, when they want. This condition affects your heart rate and brain activity. There were high levels of reported increase of stress levels if they were not able to get online. Many more people paid more attention to their Blackberry than their partner. The resultant loss of web activity at home was viewed as being worse than being without electricity itself.

I found a quote from David Lewis, psychologist, who confirmed, *"Broadband has meant we have entered a culture of instant answers, a galaxy of information is just a mouse click away. The growing obsession with the net is having a negative impact on health."*

So, between the two of us, Diane and I had broadly carried out the research required for this paper but we had to conclude in a way that wasn't going to ensure people ran off into the corner and cried. Diane decided she would read the paper with no slides and then at the end of it congratulate the group for sitting there for 15 minutes listening to her without even looking at their Blackberrys or a screen or any paper.

After the paper was prepared Diane wrote the conclusion.

She felt technology may provide the opportunities for forward-thinking law firms and individuals to diversify their practices nationally, internationally and into various areas of law which were traditionally monopolised by other service providers. Due to the increased investment in management, the time and skills labour which is required for the development of new IT (the change in the infrastructure of the firm and programming systems integration), the best opportunities may seem likely to be limited to larger firms which are able to devote sufficient resources (financial and labour) to such projects. However, she believed there to be significant opportunities for smaller firms practising in niche areas if they were prepared to devote time and commitment to developing their technological strategy or indeed if some were able to get together to share access.

She concluded the 21st century lawyer in a legal practice must work out which areas he/she needed to invest in to help their business. A failure to invest has had a serious effect on the growth of smaller firms, and with the current economic climate the combination has meant that many firms have fallen by the wayside. If they do not have good systems they may not have been able to secure indemnity insurance and therefore were forced to close. We just have to look at the increased number of firms which have a

Kitemark on their letterheads to say to the outside world: we have technology to assist us in our service to you as we implement these systems for your benefit and if we did not, we would not have the Kitemark!

Technology, Diane concluded, was an invaluable tool to be used by the legal profession. It was also debatable that in the next decade technology within the legal sector would flourish even further, to a point of no return, and perhaps play a more masterful role within the profession.

So the lesson to be learnt, she felt, was that yes it is a tool but don't let it be your master. Secretly she felt… too late!

CHAPTER 9

What's your dominant need?

It's 2011. Francis and I have been together 26 years. I would have got less for murder!

We have had our ups and downs over the years. The arguments have been based mainly on culture and choices for our children and our legal careers. We have broadly agreed on the same principle that when you pick your life partner or business partner you should adopt the same or similar methodology and not jump into things without proper thought. Remember Mr Hurst's six Ps: Proper Preparation Prevents Piss Poor Performance. Also we agreed a long time ago never to go to bed on an argument.

Before we married in 1990 we made a list of what we felt we should look for in a life partner. We then merged our two lists. Diane and I had discussed my list when she was about to open her firm all those years ago as she was fascinated by the human personality and how we can all live together – or not as the case may be.

Whilst cleaning out the joint office at home, daydreaming that I am approaching my 26th anniversary year of meeting Francis (our marriage is shorter) there is a lot of old stuff that I have come across in this office. I refer to it as a joint office as it is shared with myself and every other member of my family, including Bella, the family pet Labrador who hides in there to sleep when the family noise gets too much for her.

I came across the six needs list. Crikey, this thing is years old and it is still as relevant today as it was then! With Diane's additions made when we discussed it way back when, I am now reading the list with fresh eyes. I wonder whether Diane's list would be the same today. Mine would.

The first or perhaps main consideration was to work out what your partner's (life and business) dominant needs are. Francis and I love to discuss psychology as Francis felt he was an amateur psychologist anyway and he believed there were six core needs of any individual and that each individual had a dominant need out of the six core needs. This would be the same even if the individual concerned had an alter ego, i.e. an actor. The core person still remains. The list can be applied to any situation whether it is a life partner, business partner, friend or staff member.

I am sorry if I am going to sound like I am lecturing or presenting to you, but my semi-legal mind knows no other way to explain Francis's crazy view of the six core needs.

The first need is *certainty*. Everyone requires certainty which includes security of your family, security of your office, security of your business, survival and the ability to put yourself in a position where you actually avoid negative influence such as pain, suffering and discomfort. I need to know that when I come home my children are safe and healthy, and my husband will be in employment and happy so we can pay our bills and live our lives. Bella needs to know, and reminds us constantly she must go out first thing in the morning and last thing at night otherwise she leaves deposits in the house! Diane agreed but felt that in business certainty, this took on a different angle and the employer needed to ensure that his/her employees were comfortable and lived in the knowledge that if they did a month's work, they would be paid accordingly.

If we consider certainty, we must also consider the opposite: *uncertainty.* An unquantifiable amount of uncertainty is good and this will include a challenge, a surprise or variety which they say is the spice of life. If there is too much uncertainty in your life this can be destructive. Francis is erratic and incapable of making a decision – however, I am not. So the uncertainty in which he likes to live his life doesn't destabilise our relationship because I am the constant that ensures his uncertainty is kept in check. He would probably make a very bad businessman but as a partner he constantly surprises me in a good way with flowers, small gifts, messages, notes on the fridge and so the uncertainty of what he does next spurs us on. In a professional relationship there will be obstacles such as staff, cash flow and the recession which could make for an uncertain time. But uncertainty can be good if it adds adrenaline. In business, business owners must think of new and novel ways of transforming their business to keep up with outside influences. This can be a good thing in a business partnership and is ever present in entrepreneurs.

The third core need is *significance*. Everybody wants to feel important and wants to be made to feel important but as with certainty, significance must be the right type of significance. Significance cannot border on arrogance where you fail to recognise the needs of your partner and act like a sociopath. A saint for instance may be viewed as having too much of the right type of significance that the majority cannot attain. They constantly think of others and may as a result lose/forget themselves. A dictator has too much of the wrong kind of significance and fails to think of others.

Significance is very closely linked with the fourth core need of *love and connection*. We need to have love and connection in our home and family relationships but also there must be some sort of connection with your place of work and your business. You must have a relationship whether it is clear cut in a business sense of employer/employee or private relationships of husband/wife/life partner. If there is no connection to the business/relationship, you won't protect it, you won't allow it to grow, and you won't give it its food to live, which in a business is its employees' resources/clients to make it profitable. A business requires good management otherwise the staff have no connection to the business and all they will do is carry out their tasks in a mundane manner. They won't think about what they are doing, they won't care about their future; they won't care about the future of your business which will result in a negative culture.

If I did not care about Francis we wouldn't try so hard and we have had our periods where not only do we not like each other, we are not even on speaking terms during the day, but eventually we agree to disagree because the core love and connection is there – and we have our pact not to go to bed on an argument.

The reason Francis and I have stayed together this long is mainly because we allowed each other to contribute to the growth of our relationship which is still changing even after 26 plus years together.

The fifth core need on the list was therefore *contribution*. This is important in business and private, and relates to the giving, receiving, involvement and inclusion of your partner. If we aren't given the opportunity to contribute to our private relationships, those relationships will die. Exactly the same can be said in a business relationship. In order to help staff with the concept of love and connection to their employment/employer, they need to be able to contribute or to be seen to be contributing. Francis and I have often adopted strategies to ensure that we continually contribute within our relationship and that the children contribute in relation to our family decisions. The last Friday of every month we have a Chatham House Rules Dinner. We have been having this since the children were young. We are able to let each other know any concerns in the family and as a group we try and resolve these issues without blame. It is exactly the same in business. Staff members must be encouraged to contribute freely and the information not extracted from them.

The last identifiable need is *growth*. This could refer to the achievement in your business, going forward in the right direction as a couple and onward progression. It is a need in forward movement. If you continually grow without contribution you will leave people behind.

Francis firmly believes we all have these six core needs in us but one is more dominant than the others. I did not always see this but I have been convinced over the years by Francis and his amateur psychology! The key is to understand the paradox between certainty and uncertainty where you must get the balance correct to the same extent as using an equaliser on a stereo system. Significance, love and connection and their success depend on how you obtain that significance. It must be positive and it must be filled with love and connection if it is to work.

As I read this list in the study, it is now flooding back to me and I remember the conversation with Diane quite vividly as we went through the list all those years ago. In business Diane enthused that in addition to the six core needs, she felt there were several other main points that she always tried to explain to younger solicitors to take on board when they were looking to progress either to senior associates, junior partners or equity partners. Business relationships must be entered into in an open and frank way which means there has to be an open dialogue from the beginning, the middle and the end. Whatever discussions you have at the beginning must be precise, clear and documented. You must be able to have a document that you can all (the partners) live with so you don't slit your wrists if anything goes wrong and you can ease your way out of the partnership if necessary. She felt that as lawyers we advise our clients about business relationships all the time so, why should we not take our own advice?

Diane reiterated the six Ps that she was taught way back by Mr Hurst: Proper Preparation Prevents Piss Poor Performance. She had scribbled this on my list with the same recognisable dodgy handwriting which looks as if a spider had dropped in an inkwell and walked across the page!

I stop reading the list as I am brought back to the present day and realise why I came in here to be in the office in the first place. AD has a new client, two criminal practitioners who wish to open a practice – very brave I think. They do not have a commercial bone in their joint bodies but they don't need to. They are doing the sensible thing and having an office manager who is a retired criminal practitioner who will be able to give an oversteer on the practice. Although it is Saturday afternoon, the house is quiet. Francis is out with Baby Boy and Bella is fast asleep in the corner of the study on a chair, wrapped in towels as she has just had a wash. I moan that she never uses the bed we have for her. The three older children are nowhere to be seen. I decide I may as well make a start on the advice as dictated by Diane. I have been using remote digital dictation for years and so can type up what I receive from home and Diane's advice was framed as follows:

The first page referred to the six needs which makes me smile. After all these years she still remembered word for word. She would never tell Francis he was right but the fact she uses the analogy is testament to the fact she believes it anyway. She asked the prospective partners to be honest about their individual needs and the needs of each other, to write them down and exchange the list with each other in three days' time.

Her second point was for them to consider the term of their partnership. Did they want to go into this business relationship as a short-term quick fix or a long-term plan, in which case where did they see themselves in five, 10 or 15 years' time? They shouldn't feel the need to set something up because it is a flash in the pan as it is too important to get wrong. If things go belly up it could take years to unravel.

Thirdly she asked them to consider each other's values and ethos and if these were the same for both partners. Being a solicitor, you are obliged to follow the rules of professional conduct but because you are being asked by the wider society to act in a businesslike manner, what are your business values? She questioned whether they sat firmly with the business partners to allow the practice to move in the same direction and would they be pulling at each other which would destabilise the relationship going forward and possibly for ever.

She asked the prospective partners to put their ideas down not only in a partnership agreement but also a business plan. She implored them to consider the type of hours that they both wanted to work, the amount of billing they needed to achieve, the break-even target and to split the work, administration and marketing equally: what, she asked them, would be their core business culture? She then asked what were their core skills that they would bring to the partnership in terms of work, money, time and imagination.

As I am typing this, I realise I agree with what she has said but the fourth point took me by surprise. She felt that the partners should consider conflict resolution. *What,* I thought, *that's a bit off the wall.* Although this is important, it is very difficult to establish at the beginning of a relationship. Diane asked the prospective partners to create a questionnaire to be answered by all of the partners and which could also be used for partners and fee earners who would join later. She urged them to consider not only their dominant need but how their business partner dealt with resolution in their personal and professional life and whether or not it fitted with the other(s). Business is stressful and running a criminal practice is like no other service business in that you need to service clients to bring more business in. How will you behave in times of stress? Diane wanted them to tease out these questions in order to give the partners an indication as to how the prospective partner may behave if things go south, as everyone can behave well when things are going great but if things turn sour that's when you see the true individual come through.

Her fifth consideration was to ensure the partnership deed was prepared and that it should be easy to run the business but also relatively painless to leave. You don't want to create an impasse between the parties which would end up in court and so she was urging the parties to consider their exit strategy which allows them to walk away on speaking terms.

The sixth consideration related to the capital contribution into the business so that the firm could continue for at least six months without having to bill clients. If you expect to receive fees on the first day that you open you may be surprised that it actually takes time to do the work and then wait to get paid. If you haven't got proper systems in place this could be a shocker.

If partners are contributing, will it be the same amount in financial terms or will one be providing the money whilst the other provides the work? How are they going to do this? You need someone to work in the business and someone to work on it. Both are essential for the growth of the business.

In addition, had they prepared a SWOT analysis of themselves and the partnership?

The prospective partners were asked to consider their individual USP (Unique Selling Points) and how this would work within the practice going forward. She wanted them to consider this exercise as she wanted them to take things quite slowly. Although they felt they had a good business idea and relationship and had accumulated a lot of clients and client contacts who had helped them in their professional careers going forward, she still wanted them to take a breather and not to jump into things as she asked them to consider their relationship.

- Was the relationship based on a real assessment of trust or just an emotional connection?

- Could they trust each other?

- How long had they known each other and did they have examples of their behaviour in the past?

- Did their partner consistently meet their commitments professionally and personally? If they don't, were they prepared to do the job for them in order for the practice to continue?

- What are their positive and negative attributes?

- Which outweighs the other?

- Will they always do the right thing legally and professionally when not convenient or profitable to do so?

Once all of the above questions were answered, Diane asked the prospective partners to document their responses which she would use as a basis for a partnership deed.

The partnership agreement must be in writing and not only should it be based on the above points but she asked them to consider what would happen if one of them passed away. Would the passing mean the partnership would survive the death of the partner? Would you require a buy/sell clause funded by life insurance? Would their respective executors want to participate in the business? What would happen if disagreements ensued? Consider the personal debt of your partners: would this affect the profits of the firm? As both prospective partners were married, Diane wanted them to consider, which was very painful and embarrassing, what would happen if either of them divorced? Would the divorce settlement include the partner's share in the partnership, and further, what would happen if one of them became incapacitated so they couldn't physically get into the business premises? She suggested key man insurance.

By the time I finished typing the letter I was sure I wouldn't want to go into a business relationship/partnership with anyone for all the tea in China, and if you were, it is clear Diane felt you must do the due diligence *before* you go into business as opposed to it being a work in progress once you are there.

She finished off the advice by providing a discussion surrounding finances, tax and Solicitors Regulation Authority obligations about how they were going to collect the debt, if any, from unpaid bills. She advised on the legal issues and whether or not they wanted to open an LLP partnership or an Alternative Business Structure with a potential funder of the business. She also urged them to look at their business structure and operations and lastly to ensure that they complied with the regulations of professional conduct. I was left thinking that she gives good advice but does she follow it herself?

All in all, I felt it was a good advice letter but it does make me stop and consider what is happening with AD itself.

With the increased length and dips of the recession, the staff were asked to take half pay which caused no end of consternation. It was felt by the staff that the partners were not communicating well with the staff or indeed with each other. Although the partners' personalities were different, provided there were no external factors they appeared to work together. But with the recession continuing as long as it had been and the resultant loss of some significant cases which had hundreds of thousands of pounds worth of work in progress which were never recovered, cash flow was tight. Due to these external factors, the partners were retreating to their respective corners and cracks were beginning to show.

It was becoming apparent that the partners could no longer meet in the middle as even the middle was too far apart. If only Diane had taken the advice that she was now giving to clients on what should be done prior to the setting up of a practice, things may have been very different. Hindsight is just that after the event.

I felt it was my turn to advise Diane on what she should do as it was clear to me that she needed to sit down and do her own SWOT analysis – both personal and professional. What were her strengths, the strengths of the business, the weaknesses of both, and the opportunities and threats? The partners both needed to look individually and generally at market forces and be honest with themselves on where the practice was going and whether they needed outside help to change the internal structure and culture at AD. There were three main things that I could see they were losing: control; they weren't managing change; and they weren't as they had been previously. I suspect the recession and increasing needs for cash flow concentrated their minds elsewhere.

I advised Diane that in order to control her business she needed to understand it fully and manage it. She needed to maintain control. There was also control of the business model and the finances which were going out of the window because of the manner in which litigation funding was moving to After The Event insurance and Conditional Fee Agreement markets. This meant cash flow was hurting. Staff were beginning to feel that maybe the partners did not understand their situations. I witnessed staff becoming more insular and thinking of themselves only with no connection to the business and, correspondingly, the partners becoming more aloof. As a result there was a mismatch in expectation. With the introduction of a practice manager it is always a good idea to introduce a trusted lieutenant, but if the two leaders have very strong personalities, which way will that practice manager act in accordance with the rules? Even trusted lieutenants tell you what you want to hear even when you have not done something right!

The situation was changing rapidly outside as the recession continued and the credit crunch and associated recession wiped out billions from the fortunes of Britain's richest thousand people. It was important they could see that the current climate didn't frighten or destabilise firms. But it is clear Diane and her business partners failed to change themselves and their business. It was clear that AD had good staff but they were not investing the time and energy and capital to keep going. You are not going to spot everything and anything in your pathway and you must analyse what is important, what is less important, and delegate so that you have the ability to see and pre-empt dangers in the downturn and opportunities with staff, business and new markets.

The number of partners at AD had reduced in the practice over the years which meant that the two partners just could not cope with what needed to be done. There are three types of managers: those who see things happen, those who watch things happen and the third lot who ask what the hell has just happened. It was clear the practice was still run well from a regulatory point of view but were they all seeing the same thing and moving in the same direction? Observation only comes with time, longevity and experience and knowledge of yourself, the market, your staff, your mistakes. You can't do it without attention to detail and at this time there were only two partners at AD which resulted in too much detail with not enough time for either of them.

Now I know what you are thinking, this is all a bit too blue sky for a PA. Possibly, but I am a lawyer by training and have worked at the coal face and taken minutes for highly confidential meetings. My experience was and still is invaluable which is why my friend Diane trusted me so much. I was a real buffer and could help firms/practices to grow. There could be a real consultancy opportunity here for Diane and me if things at AD go south!

Reflections/ Lessons Learnt from the Book of the Bleeding Obvious

LAW REPORTS

LAW REVIEW

CIVIL LAW

LEGAL DICTIONARY

It is now approaching summer 2012 and we are all getting ready to enjoy the Olympics, the media has whipped us up with talk of security and empty seats. I know it will all turn out all right as I can see a media spin a mile off.

Francis Junior decides he wants to study law… for the love of the Crucified Saviour! It's not bad enough that cracks are showing at AD and I am not entirely sure of its future, and further, Francis is still reeling from the effects of losing his job again. At least he made one confirmed decision. He had decided to enrol himself on to The Book Midwife course to write a book. He believes the trials and tribulations of a male living in the UK from African parents, the son of the fourth wife of a Nigerian Chief who is a Prince in his native country by virtue of his dad, but a pauper in the UK, had a lot to say. He always wanted to write and therefore feels that the course is the way to go.

He is booked on to the next retreat for the course and although it is a daunting task I don't believe we have the funds to spend on this exercise. Unbeknown to me, Francis decides against his better judgment to place a secret bet on a horse. He did not tell me but when the nag romped home and he was several thousand pounds the richer he said he was going to blow the funds on a book writing course. I didn't want to think how much he had put down in order to win thousands. I wasn't sure if I wanted to hug him for his good fortune or slap him for being so stupid with the family finances!

I sit there looking at him swallowing air like a fish out of water. We have always tried to be honest with each other and work together where possible. We were not poor but we were rich in our family life. We had each other and our children who had never brought the police to our doors or given us any real cause for concern. They had never been involved in drugs or gangs. They were respectful towards their elders and our family and they all looked after Baby Boy as if he was their own child rather than their baby brother. We were blessed.

It is therefore with my blessing that I said to Francis to go on the course. I started to do remote working at the weekend and in the evenings using the AD systems to earn some extra money. It made me tired but needs must.

The Book Midwife professes to allow you to have a good first draft of your book within 90 days. Francis does the course, does what he is told to do and lo and behold his book is ready to be edited and is eventually published in winter 2012. He called the book *The Mind of an Entrepreneur* because he secretly felt he should have been a businessman but followed the legal route because that is what his father wanted him to do, but he has never really wanted or been really happy to do so. He was always trying to please his father. There were many sons before him. His father was quite senior in age when Francis was born and Francis has always felt that he never really had a close relationship with him but was expected to do as he was told. It is a shame he never had that close father/son relationship nor indeed with any of the numerous uncles on his father's side.

I did not believe he would be a good businessman in reality as he was far too erratic and incapable of making a decision. But he would be able to theorise for days and write a good book on what should be done with ease!

Quite surprisingly, the book sells and he used his very wide and considerable network of client contacts, colleagues, friends, acquaintances, family members and the internet to sell his book. He has been a wretched pain to live with for the several months it took for this book to be written, edited and published but it pays off. He has his launch party at the Law Society as he managed somehow through his membership of a Law Society group to secure the Reading Room for the event. The place is full, he takes loads of questions and before the end of the night he has sold every single book that he has brought with him. He then with his IT skills decides the best thing to do is to put the book on the internet and therefore does so through Amazon, and with some cute marketing tricks it becomes the Number One best seller that week.

I can't believe months ago we were worried as to where our family was going and now Francis has become a best-selling author. He is telling everyone and anyone who will listen to him how brilliant The Book Midwife course was and that everybody has a book within them. I am sure these are not his words!

As with most things in life, when everything appears to be going smoothly the inner voice in your head then wonders what the hell could possibly go wrong. I never got the feeling anything catastrophic would go wrong but Francis Junior just announced he has applied to read law at Birmingham University and he needs our help to find accommodation and to provide financial support during this time. He has applied for a loan but doesn't think it will be sufficient for him to live on. The royalties from Francis's book barely cover the cost of the drafts, his time and our living expenses. It really is the second book, once he is established, that would probably be the better sell.

Notwithstanding, we ask every single family member and family friends to contribute. Francis Junior prepares an email that is sent to all of my contacts both in the UK and abroad where in it he explains he has the taste for the high life but the pocket for a low life. He has no money. I ask for a contribution towards Francis's fund, "I ain't too proud to beg." We specify £250.00 per family; however, we receive £250.00 per person and Francis Junior's fund is at £15,000.00 very quickly! He has already received his place at university and was successful with his grant. It is therefore a surprise when he comes to me and asks me to bank his fund and only to give him £5,000.00 per annum split over the three terms of £1,666.00 per term to supplement his loan. As I look at my first born I am bursting with pride as most kids of his age would have taken the money and spent it within the first term or bought a fancy car. The moral of this story is if you don't ask you don't get. When your back is against a wall, luck can be found in very strange places! Also, if you have to beg, do so. It was for a good cause – my son.

Francis Junior comes back home over the Christmas period of 2012 and after only a term at university he is unsure of the virtues of being a lawyer. I laugh as he already has this superiority bug that lawyers have whilst at university. They think because they are studying a law degree they are somehow better than everyone else because *"we know the law!"* Bollocks! He doesn't know jack at this stage and I don't have the heart to tell him otherwise.

He explains that there are a number of oversees students who are very confident that the skills obtained in the UK would be of benefit in their home countries. They will be returning to various parts of the Commonwealth and not remaining in the UK after qualification. Francis Junior is concerned with the home-grown talent and needs a lawyer to explain just how the land lies to himself and his colleagues. Unbeknown to me, he asks Aunty Diane if she could speak with them and mentor them throughout the year. This quietly upset Francis Senior as he thought his son would come to him first.

Diane is aghast. She barely has time for herself these days but agrees that she will host the group at her offices over the Christmas period for no more than three hours max and she will provide refreshments for them. Provided the group is no more than six, they will have three hours of her time to ask any questions they want. It is the first time they will get to see a lawyer for free so they had better use the available opportunity wisely!

Francis Junior gets his group together and on the mentoring evening they all descend on the offices of AD for the meeting with Diane.

She welcomes them all and then proceeds to preach from the *Book of the Bleeding Obvious* and that there is nothing which is too complicated and what you need in law is common sense but she appreciates common sense is not common!

I am asked by Diane to take notes of the meeting as she believes it will be very useful background information as she is thinking of writing a book herself – haha! She always has her eye on something. One of the group is a rather shy-looking Asian boy from Edgbaston who had travelled to London for the meeting. He is more interested in the pointers of success that Diane believes she has achieved during her time at AD. You can see he is interested in the business side more than anything else. I laugh as I am reminded of the Asian law students of over 30 years ago in Wolverhampton. As Diane has always been interested in the business side of law itself, she answers his questions as honestly as possible.

Firstly, she says you don't know everything in your life so you must get a mentor. She told the group that she didn't want to enter into any formal or informal arrangement with emails or telephone calls going forward with any of them. She made it clear that after today she didn't want to hear or see any of them again just by virtue of the fact she doesn't have the time and would feel guilty if they had asked, so don't. But she did recognise the need for the session.

In her career, she explained, she was a serial mentee because there is no one person she wanted to get advice from but there were facets of various personalities that she liked and she tried to mould into her own personality. You can behave in a particular way that may suit you. You may find a colleague who is very funny and you wished you were more like them. You could try to be more outgoing.

You may find someone who you think is a good public speaker, then get some training. These are the sort of things you may need to do to develop the art of business as it is applied to law. We are professional business people, she said. We are also sales people which not all lawyers accepted but Diane believed we were. Lawyers are selling their service and she explained the need to create your own USP and work out what made you different from the person next door to you. It is exactly the same as a fruit seller in the market. Why would someone buy fruit from one store as opposed to another? It's in the banter – the sales pitch.

Secondly she confirmed that the business of law requires owners to be entrepreneurs and not just lawyers and you must:

a) **Take your own advice but do not believe in your own hype.** It is all very well and good being full of advice about business and entrepreneurship and she calls upon Francis's book *The Mind of an Entrepreneur* at this point which makes Francis Junior giggle. If you are prepared to advise people, be prepared to take that advice and don't believe in your own PR. It is not by chance that business leaders and entrepreneurs are drawn towards what Diane describes as the flame of publicity. AD had two partners for most of its life but had always presented itself as being bigger than that because they were able to use PR to their benefit. Some business people/professionals may have a mental illness as yet undiagnosed. Read Dr David Owen's book *In Sickness and in Power.*

b) She is clear that **in order for you to know where you are going you need to know where you came from and not to beat yourself up about things that happened in the past**. Sometimes it was those very difficult and trying beginnings either as a child, at law school or during your articles that can make or break you. There is something in your belly which makes you want to succeed and which makes you different from others. However, there has to be a burning desire within you. Entrepreneurs have something of a need to prove themselves which in itself can be a motivational force as they continually push themselves further to succeed but at what point do you stop? Business has fewer regulatory boundaries than the rules of professional conduct and perhaps never the twain shall meet! If you put a brake on yourself too early you may not grow as a business but you can't afford to take risks as a solicitor.

c) Diane felt that **you must come to terms with the fact that some people are lucky and that luck can in many instances play a part in your success** in your business as a lawyer and a person. Some things are predestined but some are also down to your own abilities and skill. Some people are just in the right place at the right time. Just as some family members (and you know who they are) are always in trouble with the law and always in the wrong place at the wrong time. Diane recalls a story of receiving some advice from a colleague who was a director of a housing association. He helped AD secure a contract with a housing association for legal services even though they were a small firm. Diane was in the right place at the right time. She took her colleague out to lunch and he said he did not want anything other than her thanks and her assurance that she would also help someone else for no fee as he had helped her. If she comes across someone who just needs that little extra push and she can pass on her good luck, she has always remembered that and been thankful for people like him who just wanted to connect. He is a real connector. If you accept that luck is part of your success, you have also got to enjoy that success. You need to enjoy the fruits of your labour and if you are working 24 hours a day you are not going to enjoy anything. You need to curb the need for more and more and more. There are only so many cars you can drive, so many houses you can own. Just remember, there is someone else somewhere in the world who is richer than you! She reminded the group that the credit crunch cut trillionaires to billionaires, billionaires to millionaires, millionaires to middle income, middle income to paupers overnight. You must have the ability to see that things can shift quite quickly and you could gain a lot but also lose a lot very quickly.

d) Diane wanted the group to **believe in the 'miracle of the mundane'** (she borrowed this expression from someone else). Detail is critical and perhaps the most critical aspect of law. As you progress, you must always remain involved in the detail of the business. It is the only way you can ensure that people are doing what they should be doing and you maintain control of your staff and business. You need to keep a grip on what you know and what your original business model was and don't deviate if at all possible.

e) Diane asked the group of baby lawyers to **always keep an eye on profits not turnover**. Make sure that the service you provide is sufficient to ensure you are able to pay all of your overheads. It is no use having too many cases you can't handle if you are making no money out of any of them. It is also great to be a billionaire or trillionaire on paper, but without real profits you have no money in the bank and your business is built on nothing. The business must be sustainable on a short-term basis but the dips of the credit crunch and economic meltdown have shown that a long-term secure position needs a stable cash flow. Diane was quite assertive in that she fully believed women were better housekeepers and business people than men. Lehman Brothers, she said, would never have been in the same position they had got themselves into if they had been Lehman Sisters! She believed 100% that women were more risk aware whereas men were NOT. She doesn't want the business of law to make entrepreneurs out of lawyers and to make it so far removed from the business of law that they no longer understood how it made money. If they did get into that position, she asked them to make sure they turned over the responsibility of running the day to day to someone who knew what to do.

f) **Sadly one more business deal will not salvage a broken business model** she said! There is no magic bullet to create a solution to a business that is going down the pan. If you have taken your eye off the ball and you find that profits are slipping and you are no longer making a profit or paying your overheads, something is wrong with the business model. The business needs to be able to pay for itself. Do not get into the trap of looking for that never ending quest for a business conquest. One more deal is not going to salvage the business and may mean that you take your eye off the ball and that one extra deal breaks you. She spoke from experience where this had happened to colleagues who wanted more until the colleague stepped over the imaginary line which solicitors should not pass.

She spoke of her legacy and that she needed to build something that would last, not for her own immediate gratification but something that would last past her demise. Diane felt the steps were to be very slow but sure steps, to ensure that the procedures in place were there for the long haul and would help the business grow so that when you take small steps, if there is a failure along the way then that's fine. The business model required vision; entrepreneurs require courage and the ability to take risks but not uncalculated risks. You have to have confidence in yourself, your ability and your business model. If the business is spiralling downwards, as occurs in many businesses during the recession, this is when your courage could force you into a place where you take a disproportionate risk and, as a result, your vision becomes less focused and your confidence could turn to arrogance.

"...far too much of the money (goes) back into the business or pledged far too many personal guarantees to banks and more dubious lenders in a fraught and desperate bid to save their prize business from impending doom."

Taken from How They Blew It – Jamie Oliver and Tony Goodwin.

Phew! By the time we finished with that first question the group of six were well and truly engrossed. I am exhausted from the shorthand note taking. I know the shorthand course I did many years ago was just coming in useful but once Diane gets going, it is very difficult to keep up with her as she talks naturally at the speed of light anyway.

The next question asked was had Diane felt she had made a difference bearing in mind she was from a Black ethnic minority group, female and working class? This led on to the question of diversity (another big topic) and Diane's lessons learnt were that in law the business case must be put for diversity. She believed there must be an external validation of diversity performance to a rigorous standard within law firms. There perhaps should be a British standard Kitemark to confirm that firms were subscribing to a standard and an explanation as to how these factors could be tested objectively to ensure that firms comply. She suggested scoring systems, and certainly where suppliers are concerned, ensuring that this is consistently applied across all companies that they work with and that the test is to be objective. Subjectivity will inevitably creep in but we have to keep it to a minimum. Diane mentioned that the Women Lawyers Division, formerly the Association of Women Solicitors, was trying to do something similar with the Diversity Charter and table where their qualitative and quantitative results had to stand up to scrutiny.

In view of the economic climate it is not surprising that some professions she felt were over represented as well as some types of businesses such as lawyers. Those businesses that work well are properly staffed, have invested and are investing in their staff and clients, and will survive the period. Firms that will come out of the current climate will be bigger, better and stronger. Certainly more diverse as the traditional PMS (pale, male and stale) firm of the past will hopefully metamorphosise into a new 21st century firm. Diane was told diversity stood for:

Different

Individual

Valuing (respecting) Each other

Regardless of:

Skin

Intellect

Talent

Years

As an employer, Diane wanted to see a link between diversity and how it affected businesses and not just the development of a Kitemark for the sake of there being a Kitemark. She constantly looked at her corporate culture (internal) and AD's brand (external culture) as it would make sense to ensure that they are aligned and clearly related. If they are not on speaking terms, that is a problem. Diane gave an example of diversity from the point of view of the human brain which she described briefly as follows:

Perception is a human process and is visual and is based on what we see. Predictive coding is therefore important. This confirms why we are able to remember certain things and in order to challenge our perceptions we have to live the experience first. The brain needs to see and keep seeing and imaging such things as diversity so that it becomes trained to accept it as normal. Simple! (Summarised from the Hermann brain dominance theory.)

People with very high levels of IQ intelligence display high levels of creativity when problems are required to be solved. They are able to draw on the different realisms of knowledge. It is better to be diverse and not reject anyone's culture in the workplace as you could stifle creativity which comes from a very different perspective. Diane felt diversity equalled creative happy people, equalled work smarter, not work harder, which she felt equalled profit, and money makes the world go round.

It is imperative that within all these different business models, ideas for growth in the profession were leaning towards business professional services and that we must identify our USP. What are yours and your firm's unique selling points?

The evening went on much as before with numerous questions and answers. The three hours went very quickly but all students appeared to enjoy the session and Diane appeared to be reinvigorated.

As a result of the informal group mentoring session and the only session, Diane was asked to attend Birmingham University in January 2013 and one attendee was the Vice Chair of the Birmingham Students Law Society. He wanted Diane to give a talk to a combined group encompassing law, accountancy, business and economics among a few of the departments. It was her biggest audience ever. Who would have guessed in two months her life would have gone topsy-turvy! They wanted her to talk about some of her experiences and looking at the hurdles that she has had to jump, climb over, vault or even Fosbury Flop over to get where she was today. She was also asked to touch upon some of the potential hiccups that were likely to emerge in the near future and what she was planning to do to get round them. If only she had a crystal ball!

Before I launch into the presentation for Birmingham University, I must set out a movement Diane was trying to get off the ground and this showed that even Diane was still looking for answers, even though she was asked to give advice. It also showed she wanted continually to think out of the box she was in and this was a point she strived to get across to students and wanted to make the point in Birmingham.

As a leader, Diane had been invited to attend many coaching courses over her time. Some courses have been provided by the Association of Women Solicitors, now the Women Lawyers Division, and through the Law Society of England and Wales. Other courses have been arranged by legal course providers or friends or colleagues who have their own businesses and may have recommended Diane to a particular course, or they were running the course themselves. Diane has also used change agents or life coaches in her time and she is clear that whatever will help needs to be explored!

There are some similar trends and cycles that she believes leaders go through and, as a result, they have very similar challenges. Women in particular as a subgroup of these leaders have an even narrower view and even similar challenges that they have had to face centred around the family and the upbringing of children.

From the numerous life coaches that she has spoken to at BNI meetings (Business Network International) and executive coaches, Diane referred to her 40s as the 'RTA Stage' or 'Ring the Alarm Stage'. The alarm is to wake you the hell up!

Following on from her mentoring session to the students in December 2012, Diane was beginning to recall how over the last few months she had become quite bored with work and was lacking in enthusiasm.

Diane had no idea why this was the case and why she appeared to be lacking in energy and enthusiasm but she was beginning to be concerned around the Easter of 2012. She went to bed tired. She woke up tired and she was annoyed that she was always tired. She had little time for herself, her family and friends and she was questioning "Is this it?" Her life was in a rut and AD was sapping her energy. The recession had meant she had to continually think up ways to change the business model and move it on and to keep the business moving and staff employed when all she wanted to do was have a break and sit in the sun. She had the real feeling her current life wasn't it and she had yet to reach her full potential of what God had intended her to do with her life. She recalls she felt like Bella chasing her tail!

As a lawyer, Diane was still motivated to act in her clients' best interests but she thought how did this fit in with her life plan, her space and her future? Born in the 1960s Diane refers to herself as an Indigo baby born too early. Indigo children are a group of children supposedly possessing special traits; beliefs about the traits vary from paranormal abilities, which Diane does not think she has, to simply being more confident and sensitive, which she thinks she is. She was uncomfortable in her 40s and was turning to religion or looking for more within her life. She knew what her USP was in law but what was it in her life?

This RTA Stage was shared by many of Diane's colleagues, myself included, as we were all born within the same academic year. Ever the entrepreneur, Diane set up a support group called Women What Lunch or WWL. They met up every other month and lunch was for no fewer than three hours. Her friends felt they kept going but were aware of their unhappiness and unease only when a crisis or illness would make them stop and review their lives.

Diane often took Bella for the weekends when we were away and she woke up to find Bella in her room sniffing her face. Diane thought either she was dead or there was a funny smell coming from her. Three days later Diane was in hospital with quinsy which is also known as a peritonsillar abscess, a complication with tonsils that are left untreated. Bella had picked it up and smelt the abscess by default. Diane thought she needed a change and fast and even possibly her own sniffer dog.

The RTA Stage was often preceded by mental fatigue, emotional mood swings which were greater than a pendulum, with a perceived increase in stress and OCD behaviour at work or in a fitness regime. Diane would not be seen dead in a gym. This may be why many 40-year-olds start to run marathons, jog just to keep moving and to keep busy. Diane recognised it all around her in family, friends, clients and colleagues. The increase in stress and the changes in behaviour could lead to relationship breakdowns or indeed affairs, because of the constant need for change, change and more change. With this change you may be getting what is right for now but not what is actually right for you long term. As a result, in this stage Diane felt you daydream of a better life when all of this baggage was removed and for us Cancerians who daydream naturally all day and everyday anyway this was very dangerous for Diane. She did not want to make any drastic changes during this period as she believed anyone in that state should pause and not make a life-changing decision which would be based on an emotional response rather than lateral thinking.

It was Albert Einstein who said:

"We can't solve problems by using the same kind of thinking we used when we created them."

Women What Lunch therefore wanted to shift mindsets and perceptions.

Diane, her colleagues and some old school friends were all successful in various walks of life, they had great family and friends but wanted more. When Diane stopped to review her life she realised there was no time for herself to sit and ponder and watch TV, watch cartoons, walk in the woods, do nothing; even if she wanted to just sit and watch the paint dry she did not have time to do so.

The difficulty experienced by this group was that we were all taught how to behave from birth to our early 30s/40s. Good girls don't ask. So, if we have a problem we don't ask others to help to sort it out. Society taught us how to behave in public and in private but also put core beliefs in our heads which we had unconsciously learnt, and that included what success looked like. Looking in the mirror, Diane did not think it was what she was looking at. She felt success looked like money, travelling, restful breaks, and relaxation when actually it is not. Diane decided to set her mobile phone to alarm (excuse the pun) at 8.30am every day with the words **I Am Enough** to convince herself that she was enough. If her brain saw it enough she would start to believe it.

Diane wanted Women What Lunch to get her core friends and colleagues to recognise this phase and slow the f… down! If you did, you could then keep performing at a high level and not drop your standards, but recognising this stage was key and to recognise it was happening and remain focused during this period and not become insular and stay in the team of WE as opposed to the team of ME.

Women What Lunch started with four friends, each were charged with inviting one new friend per quarter. If you missed three sessions in a row you were not allowed back into the group for a whole year as Diane felt you needed to rethink and prioritise your life as you must be able to take time off for you. Put the date in your diary like any other business meeting as it was an appointment with yourself. Because the core group recognised what was happening, we helped each other and moved into the next settled phase more easily, and as a result our language and demeanour changed. *How long was this going to last?* I thought. Diane and I were founding members with two school friends. Women What Lunch now regularly takes over a restaurant on a Sunday afternoon, after lunch and before dinner, so we can sit there for hours and try and right the world or just our bit of it.

CHAPTER 11

Aurora

It is now the end of January 2013. Diane is preparing for her talk at Birmingham University and to help her she digs out her talk for Aurora members that she delivered in May 2004 – nearly nine years ago. It was a great night. I was invited by Diane and we travelled together to the BT Centre in St Pauls. Diane was told to get there half an hour early which she did. What she did not know was that she would have to have a sound check and that she would be miked up! The event was also to be filmed. She was told by a speech writer that you must always familiarise yourself when you are about to present a speech and so she stood in the empty auditorium before the mad rush for seats. Her reasoning, which I have to accept, was that when you actually go to stand there for real, it will be for the second time and you won't be frightened as you have been there before! It worked. I had never seen her so relaxed as she was that night.

The Aurora speech was revamped and used as the basis of her talk in Birmingham and I can do no better than to reproduce passages from the Aurora speech in full as all she did was top and tail it for Birmingham University. Although written in 2004 with the help of a speech writer, the advice is still valid today in 2013.

I dig out the speech and start to read it so that Diane can amend the references where necessary.

'But first, I have got to say it really is a privilege to be here tonight to speak in front of such an audience as you. This is probably going to sound like I'm trying to butter you up, but I'm going to say it anyway: you're the most engaging of people, that is business people, which is a group that is ever learning, ever growing and ever ready to kiss stupidity goodbye.

If you're like me, many of you women will have had to tackle some pretty stupid things in the workplace. But as a female lawyer I reckon I've had to deal with more than my fair share of stupidity than any other people group on the planet. Why? Because in a male-dominated domain like the law, a woman is perceived as less of a threat. A Black woman therefore gets to hear some things no right-thinking Caucasian male would ever dream of saying to a Black man for fear of a backlash.

Let me give you an example, way back when I found myself in conversation with another lawyer, things weren't going too bad and so he probably felt at liberty to speak his mind on a topic dear to his heart.

"Diane," he says, "you know why the England football team never achieves anything?" I looked at him, didn't give him the impression that I cared much about the answer, but he continued anyway. "It's because there aren't enough nationals playing in the starting 11." Now I knew what he meant and he wasn't exactly endorsing diversity as the best way forward for the national side. But obviously, if you have Black players playing for England, they qualify as being British if not English and could play football, right? Kind of goes with the territory. So I said to him, "Tarquin," (not his real name, but I'll call him Tarquin for this exercise) "raise your collar." So he said, craning his neck from side to side like a tortoise, "Why, is my tie not straight?" "No," I said, "it's because your redneck is beginning to show!"

Tarquin didn't say anything; he just looked at me and smiled, weakly. And that was the end of that particular conversation. We still keep in regular contact to this day, but I tell you something, I haven't heard anything else from him like that since.

What's my point? Thank you for asking, 'cos I've got several tonight. One of them is the first major point I want to leave you with tonight. It's one of the greatest truths I've learnt on my journey in business. And it's simply this: if I'm going to get anywhere in life, the smoothness of my progression hinges a lot on my attitude; that is, how I let the way I feel dictate the way I respond to people. What I wanted to do was play ten-pin bowling with Tarquin's head. But what I did instead was deal with the situation in a way that meant we've never had to deal with the issue of race again. The idea is to respond and not react – especially when people are being stupid, because, let's face it, there are a few folk around who kind of lean a lot that way. And maybe even me, and you, if we are honest.

I find my biggest challenge isn't trying to avoid doing something stupid for fear of making myself look stupid. My biggest hang-up is not doing something stupid in retaliation to something stupid someone else has just done first.

The issue always is how we deal with and respond to bigotry and prejudice as women. So if I hear a sexist comment or similar, I'll encourage the miscreant to stop dragging their knuckles along the ground. You see, it's important to keep things light, keep my equilibrium, but also get my point across.

Equally, if I hear someone being stupid on a much more inert level, I'll also try hard not to turn it into grounds for World War III. The moment I start spitting my dummy out is the moment I lose my self-control. And no-one – I don't care how successful they are – can ever convince me that they make their best decisions when they're ready to blow their top like a volcano.

As a manager and a business partner, I spend most of my life in relationships with people I need to get on with either because I pay them as employees or they pay me, clients, and I've found it just isn't helpful to come out all guns blazing at every given opportunity. It's amazing, but people don't thank you for it! So I've learnt that the more secure I am in myself, the easier it is to sit back and pick the fights I really need to weigh into when it comes to fighting my corner.

Which leads me very smoothly to my second point tonight; if you're going to succeed in business, you need self-belief. I'm not talking about short-sighted idiocy, conceit or sheer bloody-mindedness. I mean, you must know yourself, your strengths, know your limitations and take a chance on yourself. Why not? Problem is, we can often let our self-confidence – and this is possibly especially true for women – be compromised because of how people respond to us. And then we fall into the trap of letting our past dictate our future, as opposed to letting our past inform rather than prescribe our self-awareness.

So even though being Black can attract all kinds of ill-informed predispositions, I'm determined that the issue of my colour doesn't become a critical issue for me to the extent that it undermines my self-confidence. Why should

I submit my well-being to someone else's hang-ups?! As far as I am concerned, would you not say, I am Diane a lawyer? Me being a woman is an issue for many others, but that's their problem! All I can do is deal with me, change myself. So that's what I concentrate on and what I would ask you to concentrate on also.

I'd like to suggest – and this is my third point tonight – that successful people believe in themselves, even if experts around them can produce all kinds of evidence as to why they'll fail. And achievers are also pretty good at making sure nothing gets through their defences to undermine their determination and self-confidence. Which is what I try to do, to keep myself from being overwhelmed or intimidated by major obstacles, threatening to hamper my own progress and my business.

I've often said that the legal profession suffers from PMS: it's pale, male and stale. I have used this term numerous times in my career and sometimes it is the women who object to it. They need to lighten up. If you don't fit into the dominant culture, then sometimes you are perceived and perceive yourself to be at a disadvantage which is why some people have suggested that I'm brave launching a Black-owned commercial law firm in the White, male-dominated domain of legal land, to which I reply no, I wasn't being brave, I was just being myself. I'm a lawyer, what did they expect me to do? People ask is it any easier because we're different (as differentiation is a strategic key to positioning in business)? Well, yes, possibly, but it's also harder because we're different.

Being myself was fundamentally instrumental to how I started my own business. Let me explain and take a trip back in time. I first met my first partner at AD back in the late 80s. Before you knew it, there was a little fraternity of us Black lawyers milling about together as part of this ongoing networking scene. So one day, some of us found ourselves sitting around a table saying, "There's some mileage in launching a Black-owned – but not necessarily Black-staffed – legal practice." And each of us could see how this idea might work. So we're discussing this in more detail and suddenly a spanner in the works appears out of nowhere. Somebody said, "What would you be prepared to give up to make this happen?" And there was no one around the table, apart from my soon to be business partner and me, who was prepared to compromise on our salary and lifestyle, rent out our flats and move back to our respective parents so that we didn't have to draw a salary from the business as it got off the ground. Now how drastic is that? At 30 years of age I had to consider moving back home and as much as I love my mum, I really didn't want that to happen and to live with her again.

Now I wasn't being heroic, altruistic, magnanimous or especially virtuous. I was just being myself. If you had to charge me with something praiseworthy, then the best you could get away with would be 'sensibly cautious'. Any mother would be happy to go without if it meant her kids were fed, and I wanted, using the child analogy, my baby to live too. Losing for a short while to win in the long run just made the most commercial sense. So being myself was key to finding my way forward in business but being flexible was also critical.

My fourth point is when I first started out as a student I knew I wanted to work in the City. Everyone told me that is where you should be. But I also knew that when it came to matching the obvious demand for the stereotypical White, middle-class, Oxbridge-educated male, I couldn't compete. So I had to kick the ball around and attack my goal from a different angle. And now I'm here – but I believe in a better position because I'm a business owner. By thinking with my head, big challenges needn't become insurmountable obstacles.

Sometimes you just need to take a step back to take a step forward. And if you're flexible in your attitude and your approach to business, and are willing to wait, sometimes that 'creative patience' is the key that unlocks your dreams.

So, that was that. Before I knew it, I was handing in my notice and I remember sitting down thinking *oops this is getting serious now.* But I didn't have a lot of time to get cold feet. Just a short while later, the practice opened its doors on 5th January 1998, with work waiting for me. But it's that honesty, being honest with myself, which was fundamental to helping me to get to where I am today. Why? Because you can't make choices about who to go into business with without honesty. And choosing your business partner(s) is one of the biggest decisions anyone is ever likely to make, with potentially the most serious and extensive consequences arising from that one decision if you get it wrong. So one of my biggest points tonight is if you're going to pick a partner, please get it right!

You must trust your business partner. People often ask how much you should really trust them with and I have learnt to my peril that answer is 'with your eyes closed'. You may remember as a child you played a game where you were blindfolded, you had your hands out and your friends would steer you around obstacles. You hoped that they would not steer you into harm's way like a lamp post. You must trust your business partner with your money and your professional career. If you can't do that with your business partner, if you don't believe in them, then what's the point of going into business with them? How are you going to sleep at night if you think your partner's running around behind your back putting his or her hand in the till?

That's how a partnership should work. You should fill in the blanks for one another. If you believe in star signs, my business partner at the opening of AD was land, I'm water. He's the big picture man, I'm the detail. He works *on* the business – getting the work in, while I work *in* the business – making it happen, sorting out systems. And it works. He taught me to be positive – which is another of my key points tonight – even if you have to be positive about something that's ostensibly negative.

A few years ago, I was out late that evening and had a drink. I didn't have far to go, but I knew I was probably over the limit so I left the car at the bottom of the hill and took a cab home.

The next day, I went back to pick it up and it was gone. Stolen. I was down at the police station reporting it and being quizzed by the clerk on the desk who was a little puzzled because I wasn't spitting feathers. "You seem a little relaxed about this, madam," she said. Well sure, it was 'bleep, bleep' inconvenient and a pain to have to deal with, but I couldn't see any point throwing my toys out of the pram. I couldn't do anything about it other than not let it get to me. I had better things to do with my energy.

So sure, it's inconvenient, but the car's insured, so why worry? The insurance paid out, I banked the cheque and actually the experience did me good because I had to walk everywhere and lost loads of weight. (For those of you who know me, I was very trim back then but as you can see now, I am not which may prompt some of you to suggest it's probably time I got my car stolen again!) But going back to my point, you never know what life's experiences will bring you and what at first seems to be an ill wind might just be a cool breeze. So I try, but don't always succeed, to greet every experience just the same.

We've come an awful long way in the intervening years since AD started this business. We've launched the only Black-owned commercial law firm in the City; we carry a number of major multinational companies in our portfolio, including banks, satellite TV companies and radio stations – all served by a total of 13 staff. And not only are we practising law, but we're making it too, having just won a landmark ruling in February where for the first time exemplary damages were awarded to a frustrated tenant. Their landlord had deliberately obstructed the transfer of a lease so that he could get a higher rent from someone else.

But as we got bigger, AD experienced growing pains. This living entity that is AD was no longer a baby, we have passed the terrible twos, it's no longer a toddler and is now going to big school at the age of six. We've got to put in place procedures that help maintain the AD work ethic and values which have got us to where we are today. And this is my next point, because if you're going to grow any business, I believe you're going to have to put in procedures to make sure the corporate culture and your subsequent corporate image stays precisely as you'd like it as the business evolves.

I had been thinking about psychometrically testing staff. I want us to understand ourselves, our strengths and our weaknesses and make sure we're maximising and fulfilling our potential. I want to build something here that lasts, something that I don't want to wet nurse for the rest of its days. We must now attempt to separate AD from the partners and me because if the systems are right it should spin on its own. Something which I can be absent from for however long, knowing that it'll still stand tall and do us all proud and our clients good whether I'm around or not. You have to let your child loose at some stage – but you will still be there to help and advise.

The personal and professional development of our staff is an integral part of our success, too. I want there to be an integrity to our cohesion that also lets our staff know we fit with them, as well as letting us know they fit with us. And if we're going to build on whatever level of success we've achieved to date, then we need to be at our best and perform at levels we're happy to sustain. I remember a member of staff said AD was a shiny sports car but only a two-seater as there was only room at the top for the two equity partners. OOPPPS… we needed to change that culture and fast. The perception, although wrong, was their perception.

By the way, you may remember me saying earlier that only sometimes did I say something stupid. Well, that's not entirely true, but I'm sure you'll forgive me for such an extravagant attempt at self-aggrandisement. However, there is something revealing in my exaggerated claim to be almost perfect and it's this: part of the problem with being a lawyer is that you're not allowed to be stupid, or even make a mistake, ever. You have to be on top of your game 100%, 100% of the time, otherwise you get sued. There aren't too many other professions, other than medicine and accountancy, which make the same demands of its exponents in quite the same way. This is why I took a month off last year, to recharge. Holidays are as important to your body as food. And this is my penultimate point: namely, that when you're running your own enterprise, you will have moments of stress, because it's *your* business. And if you don't learn to take time off from it, illness will take time off for you.

The most commonly accepted definition of stress is: *Stress is a condition or feeling experienced when a person perceives that demands exceed the personal and social resources the individual is able to mobilise.* Sounds like every waking day to some people.

A stress response is part instinct and part to do with the way we think so we must be aware of its ever increasing presence in the 21st century business world for yourself and your staff.

So I wanted to take a three-month holiday independent of my partners by the tenth year of business but was not able to do so. You have to be specific and work things like this into your business plan – it's that important. Because if you spend all your time in business, when do you get time to think, dream and plan about the company? About your life? Your relationships? If you're busy, busy, busy working all the time, don't be surprised if the next thing you know is that you've got staff turnover every five minutes, your service is poor, you've got more bad hair days than you can shake a mop at, and the end result is you're not happy!

When I first started at AD I was in the office nearly every weekend – seven days a week, 52 weeks a year. It was just bonkers. The partners did all the typing, the filing, research, preparing case notes, everything, as well as practising law. It was mad.

Within weeks we had to bring someone in to put in systems and procedures, answer the phone, open files, etc., which meant that we were freed up to do more and get more work in. We soon plugged that hole very quickly. Shortly after that, we realised we needed two secretaries, then two trainees, which meant we were then too big for our existing office and had to move.

So it went on and now we are about to move again. We just agreed terms on another relatively short-term let still in the heart of London's legal land. The point is that the business is perpetually moving and this living entity continues to have growing pains that need to be attended to.

Why office space on a short-term lease? This brings me on to my last point I need to make tonight. I bump into too many people who go into business wanting the world to be their oyster and they want everyone else to know it too. So they get the most prestigious premises, in the best location, on a 10-year lease. Which earns them all kinds of grief when they have to try and sell the lease to move on to bigger and better things, or find they've got a massive albatross around their necks if things go badly and the business goes belly up. So I figured that when the time's right to trade up, on a short-term lease we can afford to move if things are going well, but if, God forbid, it isn't, we can cut our losses without having to cut our wrists.

And to make doubly sure we don't court disaster unnecessarily, we get our own solicitors to do the legal work when we move, because the cobbler's children always have the worst shoes, know what I mean? Get advice. Don't be complacent. If you're branching out, there are two things that can cost you a lot of money: staff and premises.'

It's scary as I think now in 2013 how far AD has come and we both have gone in our personal and professional lives. All we need do is update some jokes in this speech and it is as relevant and accurate for Diane today as it was nearly nine years ago. As I am sitting on the train going to work for reasons best known to me, I get out a pen and paper and make a list of life lessons. I manage to somehow get to 30 before I get off the train and walk towards the office.

CHAPTER 12

Fionnula's Life Lessons

As I am on the train and will soon approach Chancery Lane, my expanded list of pearls of wisdom was fairly full and these were as follows:

1) Life isn't fair, but it's still good. I wanted to be a practising lawyer but had my family instead. That may not be fair to me but I have what a lot do not have.

2) Life isn't fair – don't get mad, get even. Diane used to say this to her family clients. I think Mrs Trump coined it.

3) Live your life to the fullest. No comment.

4) When in doubt don't fuck about. I hate indecision as Francis has learnt to his peril.

5) Life is too short and guess what? It isn't a dress rehearsal so enjoy. When you pass 25 the years feel as if they are only six months. You celebrate Christmas and before you know it, it's Christmas again.

6) Your job won't take care of you when you are sick. Your friends and family will. Go figure. Make a career but make a life too.

7) Pay your debts and on time. Bankruptcy Court ain't no shit. Just be careful of those personal guarantees you signed as a partner or a director in an LLP – they will come back to bite ya!

8) You don't have to win every battle, just win the

eventual war and stay true to yourself, in focus and sane.

9) Spend time with the people who see your tears and not only those who see your laughter. Do not run from family. They are the only ones who will put up with your childish shit.

10) Don't put things away for a rainy day. It rains most days in England!

11) Make peace with your past so it won't screw up your present.

12) Don't compare your life to others'. You have no idea what their journey was all about and their control drama. If you did, it might scare the shit out of you and you would want your life back.

13) Everything can change in the blink of an eye, but don't worry, God never blinks nor does he sleep and so you can't hide. Believe in Him whether he be Yahweh, Muhammad, Christ or Rastafari!

14) If you are about to blow your top don't speak for a full five minutes or until you trust yourself not to fuck it up. Once it is out of your mouth you can't put it back in.

15) What doesn't kill fattens. I should know. I have been overweight for most of my life.

16) When it comes to going after what you love in life, don't take no for an answer.

17) Burn candles, use the nice sheets, wear the fancy lingerie, don't save it for a special occasion, today is special. You woke up alive and every day you don't go for a dirt nap is a good day.

18) Be eccentric, don't wait for old age... as my mother has. You just get away with more when you're older.

19) The most important sex organ is the brain. No one is in charge of your happiness except you.

20) For every bad day say, "The best thing about today is it will end, in a few hours it will be tomorrow — so a new day to fuck up again."

21) Frame every disaster with these words, "In five years will this matter and would I give a shit?"

22) Forgive but don't forget — especially if you're a female and getting divorced from a cheating Bar Steward.

23) What other people think of you is none of your business, it's their drama. If you take it on you will be reactive and not be proactive.

24) Don't take yourself too seriously, no one else does — or so my siblings tell me, my sisters in particular.

25) Growing old and cranky is better than dying young and unhappy.

26) If we all threw our problems into a pile and saw everyone else's, we would grab ours back and say,

"Thank you, Jesus."

27) Envy is a waste of time. Learn to accept what you already have, not what you think you need, it is not the same thing. We actually need very little.

28) No matter how you feel, get dressed up and show up. Everyone is someone and no one is nobody. You don't know who you might meet and what they may do for you.

29) Life isn't tied with a bow but it is still a gift – it's called the Gift of Life for a reason.

30) Every once in a while say WTF and preferably with a smile.

31) Be careful, life's a bitch and then you become one.

32) May you have the hindsight to know where you've been, the foresight to know where you are going, and the insight to know when you have gone too far?

33) It is often that a person's mouth broke his nose – watch the hell what you say.

34) Be on the lookout for wolves in sheep's clothing. "No wonder, for even Satan disguises himself as an angel of light." 2 Corinthians 11:14.

35) May the luck of the Irish be with you! I couldn't finish in any other way.

Ádh mór oraibh

Epilogue

I get out of the lift on the eighth floor and the police are seizing the office computers and the accounts records. The staff are wide-eyed. The place is a mess and people are shouting at each other and at the police. As I understand it the police have a warrant to search. I am watching my life career unfold at a rapid pace before my very eyes and think *what the fuck has just happened*? It makes me wonder who will feed Bella, who will feed Baby Boy, who will help Francis as he has only just got on his feet with his own book and is writing his second. He should be earning more money but as a Black male with a Nigerian surname we know all too well how hard it has been for him and the discrimination he has had to face and why, in the end, he left law to become an author.

Life isn't fair. I thought I had my dream job and realised many years ago that things were not going as well at AD as could be but we all stuck with it. My God, I have just finished my bloody life lessons on the train. Never saw this one coming.

I walk into the reception and give a passing nod to the staff and follow the angry voices down towards the end of the corridor. I can see Diane in the corner and it is obvious there is a problem.

Later on after the police have left everything appears to have calmed down – for the moment, although there is a certain smell of desperation in the air. I knock on Diane's door and for a Black woman I can see that her face is completely white. I can see the despair in her face as she says, "Some money is missing from the fucking client account and Mark has been arrested for fraud by an abuse of position and the police have taken him away. I made the Red Alert to the Regulators and now all hell is about to break loose."

WTF!

Author Biography

Dawn Maria Dixon was born on 16th July 1966 to West Indian parents: Grace Laurencia Mendez from Trinidad and Tobago, and Calbert Dixon from Jamaica. Dawn is unmarried and has no children. She does have 2 sisters, Nola-Jane 18 years her junior who called her Mummy Dawn and Joanne, also younger but much taller. Dawn has numerous nieces and nephews who keep her busy and entertained and therefore she doesn't need her own children.

Dawn was born in Clapham, South London, and the ancestral home of the *'reasonable person'* – a concept adopted in law, but that is where the analogy stops. She was not born on the Clapham omnibus, as the metaphor states.

Dawn has an older brother Michael. She also has step-siblings.

Dawn was educated in the state system and became a lawyer in 1990. She remained at William Heath & Co and quickly became a partner in 1995, before co-founding Webster Dixon Solicitors in 1998. That firm has now closed. She now works as a legal consultant and enjoys a portfolio career.

As an entrepreneurial lawyer and former business owner, she has enjoyed wide press and attends and speaks at a number of conferences and industry events on legal issues, diversity in the workplace and women in business.

On 13th October 2005, Dawn was invited to attend the prestigious event 'Celebration of pioneers' contribution to the growth of the nation' at Buckingham Palace in recognition of her success and achievement in the legal sector, as well as her extra-curricular activities with the Law Society and organisations promoting diversity.

Dawn was given the most precious gift by her sister Nola-Jane, a pet Labrador named Bella who features as herself (the only one) in the book.